Against All Odds

The Women's Research Group

Published by The Women's Research Group
First Edition 2011

i

The Women's Research Group has been working to record the lives of women in Coventry since its foundation in 1998. It is important that the history of women in the city should not be forgotten. This book holds a variety of articles covering the whole of the twentieth century showing the struggle women had to maintain a position in the community.

Previous books published by the Women's Research Group:

Redressing the Balance
Hurdy Gurdy Days
Keeping the Balance
Telling Tales
All in a Day's Work
Making the Best of Things
Leisure and Pleasure

Cover pictures from top left:
Brenda Stone with two local nurses
Munitions worker assembling shells
Gwen (l) and friend
Barbara Davies (l) with friends at Finham Hostel

ISBN 978-0-9540604-7-3

CONTENTS

Acknowledgements

The Women's Research Group would like to thank the following organisations and individuals for their help in preparing this book.

The staff of The History Centre, Coventry, especially Rayanne Byatt.

Individuals who have supplied information and photographs of themselves, their relatives or buildings.

Disclaimer

We do everything possible to ensure that the information contained in these articles is correct. However, we are reliant upon the memories of the people we interview.

Every attempt has been made to ensure that the photographs reproduced in this book do not infringe copyright. The group has made every effort to locate all persons having rights to photographs used.

The Workhouse

Throughout our history, periods of high unemployment have always brought misery, injustice and hardships for the lower classes of society, making them reliant upon charity or state help. In early times it was to the monasteries that the unemployed or homeless would turn to for food and shelter. When the monasteries were dissolved (and before the Act for The Relief of The Poor, which was introduced in 1597) the poor and homeless were given very little sympathy. In general they were treated no better than a dog hounded from town to town and punished for being poor.

A new act was introduced in 1601 named the 'Poor Law' which categorized people into three groups. The deserving poor were those who would work but were going through temporary hardship, this group was allowed help whilst still living in their own home by receiving Outdoor Relief or Relief in Kind. Outdoor Relief was financial help, Relief in Kind provided the basic requirements such as bread, clothing, and during the winter months, fuel. The impotent-deserving poor were those who were too old or ill to work, these would receive Indoor Relief, whereby they were placed in their local Almshouse, hospital or poorhouse. The idle poor, who would not work were publicly whipped through the streets and left to fend for themselves.

This act was changed when in 1662 the Settlement Act became law and the responsibility of the poor was given to local parishes. Financial assistance was claimed from the more wealthy householders of a parish to help fund it, the extra money being raised by charging a local property tax. If they could prove entitlement to a place through birth, marriage or apprenticeship then this enabled the poor and needy to receive parish relief whilst still living in their homes. It was an act which was double sided because people who had no settlement rights could be moved on from parish to parish. Over time the cost became too much of a burden on the tax contributors and it was seen as open to abuse, so a more cost effective way to help the poor was sought.

New legislation was passed in 1722 which was to change the way the poor received charity for very many years to come, it was the earliest form of the social welfare system. The new law entitled parishes to provide poor relief in specially built workhouses. The given name is self explanatory because it was intended that the inmates would work hard to subsidise the

1

cost of their upkeep.

It was a gradual process but by the late 1770s workhouses were built throughout the country. They deliberately resembled a prison, looking grim and intimidating, purposely planned as a deterrent to people seeking charity. To receive help, the poor lost not only their self respect and dignity but also their independence, which was taken away when they entered the workhouse.

After Gilbert's Act was introduced in 1782 the system was run by a Board of Guardians who had been selected from local ratepayers who in turn employed a master and matron to supervise the running of the establishment. Money was raised through using the inmates as cheap labour for local businesses; only the very old, young and fragile would be excused from a daily routine of hard toil.

In 1834 the Poor Law Amendment Act was bought in, although not stringently followed in all parishes (some were allowed exemption), in the main it required able-bodied people who were receiving charitable help from their parish to live in a workhouse. The practice had been in progress for many years but now it was law that a person could no longer receive charity whilst living in their own home. The act also allowed parishes to club together into unions, which in turn became responsible for the building of workhouses and the running of them.

It was not made easy for people to enter the workhouse. Before being accepted into the system applicants would have to put their case before the Board of Guardians to prove they were destitute and homeless. Some of the horror stories of the workhouse were such that only those in very dire straits would wish to go in one, for them to then have to plead and beg to be given help must have been very distressing.

When admitted people would have to strip and hand over their clothes and belongings, which were only returned when they left the workhouse. They would then be scrubbed clean and issued with a uniform to be worn at all times, which stigmatized them as inmates of the institution. To avoid relationships developing between male and female residents, which might result in more unaffordable offspring, all inmates, including married couples were lodged in single sex dormitories. In 1847 a new rule allowed married couples over the age of sixty to request a shared bedroom, but very few

2

unions provided this facility.

Children under the age of seven could be placed with their mother in the female quarters, while older children were separated from their parents and housed in a dormitory of their own; although from 1842 their mothers could have access to them 'at all reasonable times.' Also an 'interview' could be arranged between parents and their children 'at some time during each day'. Boys and girls had separate dormitories and each had a small outside courtyard where they could get some fresh air, but they were usually enclosed behind high walls providing little sunlight.

Education for the young was rudimentary and many pauper children were forced into apprenticeships without the knowledge or permission of their parents. The tragedy is that some children spent their entire lives inside the workhouse, some died and their parents were never informed.

In theory a workhouse was not a prison, so an inmate was free to leave at any time, but a family would have to leave together, giving the parents no chance to better themselves before bringing the children out. Also in practice they could not leave before they had received their own belongings and handed the institute's uniform back, not to do so would result in them being arrested for theft of workhouse property.

There were many rules and regulations and anyone who flouted them would be punished harshly, usually by reduction in their food ration or especially in the case of male inmates a beating to the hands or back. There was a strict code of silence imposed during meal times and no cutlery was provided to the inmates, all food was eaten by hand or supped as a broth. These rules were implemented to prevent inmates from arguing and harming each other and they were not abolished until 1842.

The poor were not criminals but their rations were less than those of prisoners locked up in gaol for committing all manner of crimes. The weekly official rations for HM prisons in the 1840s was 292 ounces of food, the workhouse diet was between 137 and 182 ounces a week, women and children received less than men. The food was very stodgy so that people required little to feel full. A typical daily diet was mainly bread, rice, potato, gruel and a small portion of cheese and meat. The nightcap was a drink called skilly which was a mixture of meal and water described as an insipid drink without any flavour.

We all know of Dickens's Oliver Twist and of course there are always exceptions to the rules, but by late Victorian times workhouses had a terrible reputation for being overcrowded, disease ridden and thoroughly miserable places to live in. The majority of people willing to take up residence were mainly orphaned or unwanted children and people unable to look after themselves such as the very old, sick and the mentally or physically disabled who could hardly work to support themselves. To end up in the workhouse became the working classes' worst nightmare.

Coventry City's Workhouse History

Coventry has a long history with the workhouse system, one of the earliest was in the parish of Holy Trinity 'in the priory' which was dated to 1613. It is also believed that one of the early workhouses stood in Foleshill, on or near the site now occupied by Little Heath and Good Shepherd primary schools. There was to be several replacements, the first around 1787 and another in 1799.

The workhouse in Coventry was made independent of all others around the country when in 1801 a local act of parliament was passed 'For Better Relief Of Poor In Coventry'. This act allowed the Coventry Incorporation to be established. To make it easier to manage the finances of the poor relief, it was decided to unite the parishes of Holy Trinity, St Michael and St John. The Guardians of the poor, elected a board of 18 directors and it was their decision to sell the existing workhouses and purchase Whitefriars House, the ruins of a former friary, and convert it into a workhouse.

The building was enlarged and the cloister walk was converted into the main dining area by glazing the uncovered windows. In 1804 all the old, small workhouses within the city were closed and inmates were transferred to Whitefriars. Between the period of 1812 and 1824 all able bodied paupers were put to work making silk fabric for a contractor who operated a silk mill within the workhouse. The directors of the workhouse received one shilling a week for each pauper employed, the paupers would receive one penny from this and a further four pennies a week from the contractor. In 1840 the decision was made by the directors that children under nine years old should not be employed in the silk mill.

Over the years Whitefriars was consistently extended as more room was needed, a hospital wing was added for the sick and a maternity ward. The workhouse system in Coventry was thought to be too soft and was criticized by the Poor Law Commissioners for being too comfortable and appealing to those looking for charity. By 1843 between 450 and 500 paupers were accommodated in Whitefriars even though the people of Coventry continued to receive out-relief, which was against the 1834 Poor Relief Act.

It was in 1874 that Coventry workhouse became a union. A Board of Guardians was appointed and it came under the national framework. Due to overcrowding, a new Workhouse Infirmary was built; it was opened on a wet February day in 1890 and was to later form the basis of Gulson Road Hospital. The Local Government Board continued until 1930 when Whitefriars ceased to be called a workhouse, although for the people of Coventry it was still a place to be avoided at all costs.

Women and the Workhouse

Life was a daily grind for the poor in the late Victorian and Edwardian times and it was especially hard for women. It was rare for a married woman to work outside her home because all her time and energy was spent running the house and looking after her husband and children. Big families were normal and wages were very low, so a woman had to be very astute with money, making a few pennies go a long way and many families lived constantly on the breadline. It only needed a minor blip in their finances to put a family into a crisis, which could result in them having no other option than to apply to go into the workhouse.

Families were especially vulnerable during times of high unemployment when a husband may have to travel many miles to find work. To prevent families using the workhouse as a convenience at such times, the rules of the workhouse stated that married women and their children could not enter the workhouse without their husbands. To get around this ruling husbands and wives collaborated together with the wife pleading to the board of governors that her husband had deserted the family. This ruse would allow the woman and her children to stay in the workhouse whilst her husband looked for work, with the full intentions of reuniting the family later.

This ploy was only one of the reasons why a woman would become an inmate of such a dreaded place. Many women and children found themselves inmates of the workhouse through death, illness or injury; other women were genuinely deserted by their husbands and boyfriends. To be a lone woman bringing up children without any state help whatever the circumstances, would have been very difficult.

It was not an easy option for a woman to go into the workhouse, for only the very old and sick would be excused from the daily tasks that were needed to be done in the running of such an establishment. Whatever her circumstances a woman would be expected to work long grueling hours doing soul-destroying jobs, the cold walls and floors had to be scrubbed and all manner of tasks were to be done in the kitchen, laundry and nursery.

Sarah

Whilst researching my mother-in-law's family history, I learned through the 1891 census that her grandmother, Sarah, was an inmate of Coventry's Whitefriars workhouse. My mother-in-law, Gladys, had been very close to her grandmother and had always felt there was something in her past that she was ashamed of. Gladys was aged ten when her grandfather died. After a while Gladys felt her grandmother was lonely so she pleaded with her parents to let her live with her. It was decided that she could stay with her grandmother during the week and another granddaughter stayed at the weekends.

Over time Gladys was to learn that her grandmother's childhood had been unhappy, and that her grandmother had always felt that she had been given away as a baby to an elderly couple who ran a newspaper shop in Coventry in the area of Gosford Street. Gladys often asked questions about her granny's childhood, but Sarah would sigh and say, 'There is very little I can tell you, I was used as a skivvy and never allowed to be a child'. Sarah told Gladys her earliest memories were a routine of meeting the early morning train from Birmingham to collect the daily newspapers, whatever the weather she would have to pull her little trolley laden with papers back to the shop, sort and deliver them all before she went to school.

Although as she became older, Gladys knew her grandmother did not like to talk of her early life she was curious and would try to wheedle information from her. She learned that when she was about eleven her grandmother was sent to live with a widow who had a son. Through research I believe this could have been her own mother, but Sarah had told Gladys that she did not think it was her real mother, because she felt her mother would not have treated her in such a way as this woman had.

I have tried to find Sarah's birth details, but to date have been unsuccessful, I cannot locate her records even though I know she was born in, or around 1870. The earliest record I have found is in the 1881 census when she was eleven years old and she was living in one of the poorest areas of Coventry in very overcrowded conditions. She was living with a woman named Annie Bisbon and her son. Annie is described as a charwoman and Sarah is recorded in the census as her daughter.

What happened to Sarah between the years of 1881 and 1891 can only ever be speculation, but after such a sad childhood she probably left home or was made homeless by her mother at a vulnerable age. She certainly met somebody with whom she had a relationship and must have been deserted by him when she discovered that she was having a baby, because whilst in the workhouse she gave birth to a baby girl whom she named Annie. Sadly there must have been many young girls like Sarah during the harshness of the late Victorian times, who through unfortunate circumstances was left with no other option than to go into the horrific nightmare of the workhouse.

Sarah was recorded as working in the laundry which would have been very exacting work, for they washed the clothes in large tubs of water heated to boiling temperatures by geysers. Mothers were not allowed to leave the workhouse without taking their babies out with them, records show that baby Annie died in the workhouse at the age of two. Sarah would have lived in the workhouse until her baby died and this must have caused her great shame for it is a secret she took to her grave.

Sarah was to find true happiness and security, when within a short time after her baby's death she married John Hayward, who was a tailor and in the 1901 census they had four children ranging from a baby son of three months to a seven year old child.

They lived in Jordan Well, in Coventry; the address indicates that they lived in a house that adjoined a shop, which suggests he worked for himself as a tailor. When I related this information to my mother-in-law she said she could remember when she was a very young child, how she would sit on a big table watching her grandfather cutting out patterns, using what was to

7

her a huge pair of scissors, absolutely fascinated.

We know very little of Sarah's tragic childhood, or of her sad days as a young woman that resulted in her entering the workhouse and loosing her first child in such an unhappy place. What we do know, however, is that she had a very happy marriage and in her later years when she needed them, was looked after by a very loving family who cared for her and about her until the day she died.

Memories of Mrs May West

May West was a nurse in the London Road Whitefriars during the war; her memories are recorded in the Coventry archives on audio tape. She tells of how she was born in Atherstone in May 1916, where her father was a foreman in a hat factory, a trade for which Atherstone was renowned at that time. Her mother was a Coventrian whose father was made a freeman of the city after he had served his apprenticeship in the watch and clock trade. May was not unfamiliar with the scars that the workhouse could leave on a family, for her mother had experienced terrible shame when her errant brother (May's uncle) had died in the workhouse.

May's childhood had been far from happy; sadly her mother died when she was seven years old and afterwards she felt her childhood lacked the love and comfort that she had received from her mother. Her father remarried, but her stepmother showed her no love or affection and May felt she was a spare part in her father's life. She believed that her up bringing made her hard natured and prepared her for the job she was later to do at Whitefriars.

Her father died in 1929 when May was thirteen and her stepmother was not at all sympathetic towards her. Although May was unhappy she lived with her and continued her education until she could move away and begin training as a nurse. At the age of sixteen she became a probationary nurse at Sparkhill Hospital in Birmingham. Her main nursing experience during her time there was with women, which was to stand her in good stead for her work at Whitefriars. She never completed her nursing training because before she took her final qualifications she married and a little later in 1937 came to live in Coventry.

At that time it was not expected that a married woman would have a job as they were expected to stay at home and look after their family. May was not a maternal person, so she got a job doing casual work in an office for an agency and also did voluntary work at a First Aid Post. She worked for the agency for a period of about eighteen months. It was in 1939 when war broke out that the workhouse premises needed staff with nursing experience, so May applied for a post there. When she went for her interview she first had to show her birth certificate at the Coventry Council House and believes that everything went through the council.

Although strictly speaking Whitefriars had ceased to be a workhouse at this time it was still run in the same vein and was still deemed a place to be avoided at all costs by the local people of Coventry. When she was introduced to Mr and Mrs Watson who still held the title of master and matron, she emphasized that they were not at all as she had imagined they would be. Whilst they were very strong disciplinarians with the patients (whom she stressed had to be, considering the type of people they were dealing with), they were very good to the staff. If any of the staff had a complaint or grievance they were quite willing to listen to their point of view and if needed take the necessary action to sort it out.

Once May was established as a nurse at the London Road Institute she was put onto shift work. There were three shifts in a day which were 6am to 2pm, 2pm to 10pm and a night shift 10pm to 6am, these were worked week about. Her main duties were in the women's ward which suited May well with her previous nursing experience. Her duties were many for she had to help wherever it was needed but in the main she cared for the elderly and sick.

She describes the patients living accommodation as very basic with little comfort and no homely touches. It was very hot in the summer but freezing in the winter, the whole place being heated by coke boilers, which had to be kept stoked up by the patients during the day and a handy man at night. Men, women and children were not allowed to mix and had totally separate living quarters. They slept in long dormitories with the beds placed in rows where there was no privacy for them, and the iron beds had straw mattresses, which were not very comfortable. The dining room was sparse with no flowers on the long tables or any ornaments. The cutlery and crockery was all specially marked for the institute and was old, with many pieces of crockery being cracked and chipped.

Meal times were kept to a strict routine and everyone ate the same unless they had medical problems. The meals were brought in ready cooked from Gulson Road Hospital. Breakfast was porridge and orange juice, the evening meal was served at 6pm and was known as high tea, which although varied a bit was usually scrambled or poached egg or kippers. May pointed out that it was wartime and food was rationed so portions were small, the inmates took it in turns to make a mid afternoon drink.

Every morning a service, which lasted about 20 minutes, was given for the patients. Although she said some moaned about going to the service, they all had to attend and sing a hymn of which 'The Old Rugged Cross' was a favourite and they would end the service with a prayer. The able bodied were kept very busy washing clothes, cleaning floors, bathrooms and making themselves useful because they had to earn their keep and being busy stopped them from causing trouble.

Many of the inmates had social problems such as alcohol dependency and many were in a terrible state when they entered the institute. May described how they would have to scrub people clean because they may not have washed for months and the grime was caked into their skin and nails. She goes on to say that some smelled so bad it would put them off their food, but they would put them into the bath and more often than not burn their clothes, or if they were not too bad fumigate them and keep them in store for when they were ready to leave the institution. Each new patient was issued with a complete uniform, which included underwear. Uniforms were all the same and this again stigmatized them.

There was an inspection every Tuesday and Thursday afternoon for head lice or nits. If head lice were found they would put a cloth compress wrapped like a turban around their head, which was soaked in sassafras. May went on to say that sometimes the patients would try to hide in the toilets or whatever to avoid the head checks because the sassafras had a very unusual and distinctive smell so everyone knew if a person had been treated. They were especially stringent with the bedridden, because fleas and nits tended to breed more quickly in those conditions.

She said a doctor would visit the institute two or three times a week to issue pills or treat those patients who needed it and the nurse on duty would give the patients their tablets. If needed there was an emergency doctor that could be called in. Many of the people were old or very ill, so death unfortunately was a part of the job. So as not to alarm people when someone died they would say, 'we are taking them to Ivy Cottage' and they would take the body to the mortuary.

When asked the average age of the patients May said they were all ages, the elderly usually came in of their own accord, whilst young girls or women were more often than not bought in by the police after the administration part of their admittance had been done. Most of them had been picked up from the streets for causing a disturbance of some kind. Many of them were addicted to alcohol or methylated spirits and some were prostitutes. Others were homeless or pregnant and some were in a terrible state and even suicidal. She said it was such a shame to see young people in such a state.

May said there were many funny incidents and some of the patients were real characters. She explained how all older women were called grannies; one called Granny Barlow had come in after her home had been bombed. She was a legend in her area and always wore a man's peeked cap, a grey padded shawl, long black skirt and pushed a four wheeled hand cart from which she sold artificial flowers. They had a terrible game trying to get her to bathe because she was terrified of water, so they always left her until last knowing they would have to drag her hitting them and spitting at them. She thought they were being cruel to her but they were just doing their job and trying to keep her clean.

Another was known as Miss James, she was about 29 and had been jilted by her boyfriend, this naturally had caused her great distress, as she could not accept it. As a result she suffered from terrible depressions and had developed a religious mania, which was very unnerving to some of the other patients. She believed everything she did was prompted by God. One day she threw a bowl of water over the granny in the next bed, soaking her and understandably the granny became most distressed and upset and caused a terrible scene. When she was asked why she had done it Miss James pointed to the sky and said He, God had told her to do it, she caused so much chaos that after a time they had to have her certified and she went into Hatton mental institution, poor thing.

Then there was Mrs Hogan who was very alert and never missed a thing; she used to put the spooks up everyone by predicting an impending death.

One old granny was very ill so her bed was screened off from the others. When they went into the ward a little later Mrs Hogan had everyone in a real state telling them the granny was dead and she knew this for she had heard the angel of death patter down the ward, she seemed to have a strange psychic gift.

May was asked if she thought the patients were happy living in there, she replied that it was not through choice that they lived there, but it was better than sleeping on the streets and they had regular food to eat. She said some did not like all the rules and regulations, but most realised that in order for the place to run smoothly and efficiently the rules needed to be obeyed and the patients needed to know who was boss. As for visitors, she said that the patients did not have many visitors especially the elderly, sometimes the younger patients may have an occasional visitor but it was not the type of place people would really want to come.

In summary, May said she felt her work was fulfilling and that if she had not needed the money she would have done the work voluntarily. She said it was not a place of work that would have suited everyone and she was sure that it was her childhood, which had hardened her nature and thus prepared her to be able to cope and deal with some of the difficult circumstances of the job. It needed a hard person to keep the patients in check, a soft natured person may have become upset and unable to cope with some of the situations she had dealt with. It could have resulted in them being taken advantage of by the patients, which would never have done for they needed discipline. When asked if she was ashamed of working at Whitefriars, May replied that although she felt no shame for the job she did, she was very aware of the stigma attached to anyone who was associated with the Institute and she admitted that if asked by a casual acquaintance where she worked she would always say she worked on the London Road.

Whitefriars showing the cloisters that were glazed to house inmates.

Whitefriars a sad ending

During the Second World War the eastern part of the workhouse was used as Gulson Road Municipal Hospital to treat wounded soldiers, whilst the old monastery became a Salvation Army Hostel, which continued to accommodate people with social needs. Whitefriars did not entirely escape the effects of the war with parts of its buildings being badly damaged during an air raid but it continued to be in use throughout the war. Three years after the war in 1948 a new National Health Service came into being, which provided free medical treatment for all, including a revised welfare state package, which was to alleviate many of the poor people's problems.

Whitefriars continued to be used by the Salvation Army as a hostel to look after the welfare of homeless people, especially those with alcohol related problems. It ceased to be used for this purpose in the early 1970s when the Salvation Army moved to new premises in Lincoln Street. The old infirmary buildings continued to be in use as Gulson Road Hospital, although some of it has been demolished, a section of the hospital is currently in use for physiotherapy and other services.

Sadly the original part of Whitefriars now stands alone and is precariously close to a heavily used section of the Ring Road. The vibration from constant traffic and its pollution are doing more damage to the last remaining fabric of the friary than anything else has during its long history.

The side of Whitefriars showing how close it is to the Ring Road.

As time goes on memories of the workhouse will fade and become more obscure but as long as the ruins of Whitefriars remain standing the scars of the workhouse will forever be visible in its thick cloister walls. The walls show the evidence of where the dining hall tables and benches were attached to them as do the upstairs friars' dormitory where the imprints of a

13

partitioned wall can still be seen running down the middle of the tiled floor. Is it too late for someone with great foresight to come up with a plan that will secure this historical building?

Bibliography

Foleshill Union Workhouse, Punishment Book 1864-1900
Distressed Weavers, Deserted Wives, Fever Cases; Analysis of admissions to Coventry Workhouse by Rosemary Hall, Warwickshire history – Journal of the Warwickshire Local History Society, Volume XIII, Winter 2007/8
Cassette PA1662/2/133 – Oral History interview: West, Mrs. M. Coventry History Centre Workhouse New Infirmary – *Coventry Standard*, 1890

Internet Sources

English Poor Laws – Wikipedia.org
Details of Workhouses – Wikipedia.org
Whitefriars Monastery
– http://www.historiccoventry.co.uk/tour/whitefriars.php#workhouse
1891 Census Records –
Civil Registration Index – Ancestry.com

You Must Use Your Vote - They Suffered For It

The struggle for women to be able to vote lasted nearly 100 years, from the first petition presented to the House of Commons in 1832 until 1928. Although in 1918 the Representation of the Peoples Act, gave women of property over the age of 30 the right to vote, not all women therefore, could vote, but it was a major victory for suffrage. A general assumption is that the act was a 'reward' for the vital work done by women during World War One. It was in 1928 when finally women were entitled to vote on the same terms as men.

During the women's speeches they often had rotten eggs and other missiles thrown at them and were assaulted by yobs and quite often the women battled with the police. They were sent to prison and suffered forcible feeding. These women were only standing up for their right to vote.

Unfortunately they had to deal with a Prime Minister like Mr Herbert Asquith, who could not understand why women should want the vote. He was not helpful towards them at all, supported by his wife Margot who was an anti-feminist. I wonder if the whole scenario would have been different if someone else had been Prime Minister, and accordingly would the ladies have had the vote earlier.

We have all heard of the Pankhurst family. In 1903 Emmeline and Christabel founded the Women's Social and Political Union (WSPU), at 60-62 Nelson Street, Manchester; this is now a museum named the Pankhurst Centre.

On the evening of the General Election held on the 13th October 1905, Christabel Pankhurst and Annie Kenney interrupted a Liberal Party meeting, which was being addressed by Sir Edward Grey at the Free Trade Hall, Manchester, by asking if the Liberal Government were returned to parliament, would they give votes to women. This was the first time the slogan 'Votes for Women' was used. Their question was not answered so they repeated it; the two women were roughly ejected from the meeting. Unfortunately, Christabel committed the offence of spitting at a policeman in the hope of being arrested. Both of these women were charged with obstruction and sentenced to pay fines or face imprisonment. Emmeline Pankhurst offered to pay their fines, which both women refused and they were imprisoned for a few days. Of course this was a good ploy as immediately it put the WSPU in the public eye and the movement began to grow rapidly. It was not only upper and middle class women that joined the movement as Annie Kenney always introduced herself as a factory girl and trade unionist.

The Pankhurst family moved to London and the WSPU began to sever its links with the Independent Labour Party (ILP). The Pankhursts and many other women were imprisoned on numerous occasions. In February 1913 the WSPU started a prolonged campaign of arson. Suffragettes smashed the orchid house at Kew, set a railway carriage alight and bombed Lloyd George's house. Emmeline boasted about it at a public meeting in Cardiff and was sentenced to three years penal servitude; she refused food, but was not forcibly fed and was released after a few days.

Many of us have heard of Emily Wilding Davison. She was known amongst the suffragettes as a 'loose cannon' and a political firebrand. She went to London University, obtained a First Class Honours Degree and became a teacher and governess. In 1906 she joined the WSPU and devoted her life and death to the cause. On the 4th June 1913, the King had entered a horse into the Epsom Derby. Chaos followed when she ran onto the racecourse and tried to seize the horse's reins, but the horse ran straight into Emily, fracturing her skull and causing many internal injuries, she died four days later at the age of 40. Most of the sympathy was for the jockey and the horse, which had to be put down. Many thousands of suffragettes said a sad farewell to Emily and they saw her as their martyred heroine.

Many of the suffragettes in the WSPU became isolated from the rest of the women's suffrage movements and became disenchanted and defected to the Women's Freedom League (WFL). They objected to the way that the Pankhursts were making decisions without consulting the members. Like the WPSU, the WFL was a militant organisation although most members were pacifists, and when World War One was declared in 1914 they refused to become involved in the British Army's recruitment campaign.

Millicent Garrett Fawcett held the position of President of the National Union of Women's Suffrage Societies (NUWSS) from 1890 until 1919. She took a moderate line of approach, and was a tireless campaigner, who was concerned that the militant methods of the suffragettes were harming the campaign. Millicent helped found Newnham College, Cambridge. Her niece Louisa Garrett Anderson was a militant suffragette who was sent to prison for her militant activities. I wonder what her Aunt Millie thought of her as she was a non-militant? Louisa was a daughter of Britain's first woman doctor, Elizabeth Garrett Anderson. Louisa was also a doctor and was Chief Surgeon at an army hospital in Covent Garden, London.

Many of the suffragettes who were sent to prison went on hunger-strike and were forcibly fed. In 1909 Laura Ainsworth and Hilda Burkitt were sent to Winson Green Prison, Birmingham, for disrupting Herbert Asquith's meeting held at Bingley Hall, Birmingham. A full enquiry was held in Parliament regarding the treatment of Laura. She said 'I was forced into a seating position, and a tube about two feet long was brought out, my mouth was opened with a steel instrument, I felt I was going to choke and a gag was placed between my teeth to keep my mouth open'.

The threat of death occurring from a hunger-strike resulted in the introduction of the Prisoner's Temporary Discharge of Ill Health Act, which became known as the 'Cat and Mouse Act' of 1913. This did not prevent women from going on hunger- strike but, as they became ill, the authorities would release them and let them return to their normal life. However, on recovery the women were re-arrested on minor charges and immediately returned to prison for completion of their sentences. Force-feeding, was no longer imposed and the government could now lay claim that any harm or death resulting from starvation was the fault of the suffragette. The women who went on a hunger-strike were presented with a medal, inscribed 'For Valour' and dated. It was attached to a ribbon containing the suffragette colours i.e. Green for Hope, White for Purity and Purple for Dignity. The suffragettes also wore sashes and rosettes in these colours.

Eleanor Rathbone was born in 1872 and was elected as an independent member of Liverpool City Council in 1909; she maintained this position until 1934. She fought hard for women's rights. From 1918 onwards, she argued for a system of family allowance to be paid directly to mothers. In 1919 when Millicent Fawcett retired Eleanor became the President of the NUWSS. In 1929 she entered parliament as an Independent MP. During the depression, she campaigned for cheap milk and better benefits for the children of the unemployed. She also fought for Family Allowances and finally won in 1945, this developed into Child Benefit. She was furious when she discovered that the allowance was to be paid to the father rather than the mother. She was also involved with women's suffrage, human rights and refugee issues. Eleanor along with Eva Hubback founded the National Union of Townswomen's Guilds. She died in 1946.

Suffragettes in Coventry

A first petition from Coventry was presented by Mr P.A. Taylor, who was a radical MP for Leicester on the 9th March 1870. In 1886 seven women signed the Women's Suffrage Petition, but none of them appears to have taken any further part in the campaign. On the 6th November 1871 Jane Ronniger (who was the Vice President of the Suffragette Fellowship), travelled the country lecturing on behalf of the London National Society, including a meeting in Coventry. By profession she was a teacher of voice and recitation. On the 10th April 1874, two members of the Birmingham Society, Mrs. Eliza Ashford and Miss Sturge, accompanied by the Central Committee's lecturer, Miss Mary Beedy who addressed a meeting in St. Mary's Hall, Coventry. At this time it appears that they could not arouse much enthusiasm from Coventry women.

Some years later on the 27th February 1890 at a meeting held in the New Assembly Hall, Coventry, Miss Chapman from Winchester addressed the Coventry Women's Liberal Association, on the subject of Women's Suffrage. The Associations president, Mrs Joseph Cash, took the chair. In June of 1890 Florence Balgarnie spoke on women's suffrage to the men of Coventry Liberal Club.

In the 19th century no branch of the main suffrage society was formed in Coventry. In 1895 Amy Hurlston was the secretary of the Coventry branch of the Women's Emancipation Union. It is doubtful that the group conducted much of a campaign in the city, but its existence suggests that there were at least a few women who were interested it its aims.

In 1908 a Coventry Branch of the WSPU was formed and operated under the control of the Regional Centre in Birmingham. In 1910 the Coventry Secretary was Miss Helen Dawson, who firstly gave her address as St. Peter's Vicarage, Hillfields, Coventry and by 1911 she was at 20 Northumberland Road, Coventry. By 1913 she had been succeeded by Miss C. Arnott of Beech Brae, Berry Street, Hillfields. For a while in 1912/13 a WSPU organiser, Miss Marwick, was based in Coventry, working from 33 Earl Street. Mrs Pankhurst visited Coventry to address a meeting at the Baths Association Hall on the 23rd January 1913 and she stayed overnight with a WSPU member Mrs Widdrington.

In 1909 a Coventry branch of the NUWSS was formed. Its secretary was Miss Wilks of 76 Holyhead Road and in 1910 she shared the position with Miss French who lived at 'Daisy Bank', Middleborough Road.

In the *Midland Daily Telegraph* dated 10th February 1939, there is an article regarding Mrs Gladys Stringer who was a former Mayoress of Coventry when her husband Sidney Stringer was the Mayor in 1938. Mrs Stringer was from Ffestiniog, North Wales and she helped the suffragettes achieve emancipation. It is possible that in the early 20th century she was in Birmingham where she met Mrs Pankhurst on numerous occasions and was in contact with other prominent members. She was definitely one of the more moderate members. In the 1920s she shared her husband's belief in Socialism and worked hard for the Labour Party. She was a welfare worker and served on the area war pensions committee until a short time before she died in 1973 at the age of 80. She was also a governor of Barr's Hill School.

She went on to say that one could not help but recall the work of the early pioneers of the old suffragette movement, and the names of local women who worked so hard and consistently for the cause. She recalled the names of Enid Stacy who was the sister of the Rev. Paul Stacy, the Vicar of St. Peter's Church, Hillfields, she later became Mrs Widdrington when she married the Rev. P.E.T. Widdrington who succeeded Paul Stacy as the Vicar of St. Peter's Church. Miss Helen Dawson who later became the Rev. Widdrington's second wife; the late Mrs. Collington, wife of Dr. Collington, who represented Hillfields on the Coventry City Council for many years and Miss Anna Oliver. Mrs Stringer was reported as saying that these Coventry women sprung to her mind. She went on to say that it took a war to convince many of the changed circumstances in the status of women, and undoubtedly the work that was undertaken by women during the war years persuaded the Government of the justice and necessity of giving women the vote. Many of Coventry's suffragettes had by the time of this interview passed away. Others had left the district, but few still lingered in the city, and sometimes dreamed of those days before the war.

There is a report in the *Coventry Herald* dated 10th February 1939 with Mrs Wanley, who lived at 58a Cromwell Street, Coventry. She said that she often re-lived the excitements and scenes of her younger days. Not that there were many excitements in Coventry. On the whole she told the newspaper that the Coventry suffragettes were an orderly body, and did not agree with the militant actions of their fellows in other parts of the country. She went on to say that nothing ever came of violence. Her memories of the suffragette movement were therefore chiefly concerned with orderly mass meetings, often held in Priory Row, occasional parades and gatherings in the Coventry District. In fact the most exciting thing that happened to her occurred at a mass meeting in Warwick. She arrived a little late and was mistaken for Mrs Pankhurst and she was subjected to enthusiastic cheering on the one hand and hissing and abuse on the other. Mrs Wanley continued that when they heard the news that the Bill had been passed there was little rejoicing, even amongst themselves. It was not the time for rejoicing as people could only think of the war. Mrs Wanley was asked if she would do suffragette work again if it was necessary, she replied quite emphatically 'I would. My husband always opposed the movement but that made no difference to me. It is only right that women should have the vote'.

Enid Stacy was born in 1868 and was a socialist and campaigner for women's rights. She was closely associated with women's rights issues but unfortunately she died in 1903 just before the suffrage campaign highlighted existing tensions between issues of loyalty to sex or to class. She was committed to the socialist cause and was praised for her skill as a speaker. Enid was different from the usual socialist women insofar as she took her views from an individual standpoint and she described the campaign for women's rights as a 'middle-class fad'. She did attend suffrage conferences to argue her case from a socialist perspective but she did not give her time to the women's movement as such.

According to the marriage certificate she married Percy Elborough Tinling Widdrington, B.A. of St. Edmund Hall, Oxford, the eldest son of Sidney Latimer Tinling Widdrington, H.M. Inspector of Customs in Liverpool. Enid was the eldest daughter of Henry R. Stacy of 18 Cotham Road, Bristol; on 29th May 1897 at All Saints Church, Clifton, Bristol.

Throughout 1913 and early 1914 there were constant reports of the activities of the suffragettes in and around Coventry. Mass meetings were held, letters in pillar-boxes destroyed by fire and authority sometimes resisted. Yet what was not to be won by civil strife was won by a world war, and then the passing of the Bill in 1918 almost went unheralded.

An article in the *Coventry Standard* dated 22nd February 1951, tells of the memories of Ex-Deputy Chief Constable – Superintendent S.B. Langford. He recalled the time the suffragettes were active in Coventry, he got hot around the collar, for he could not think of a more embarrassing period in his early days with the Force. He was only a young constable at the time it all started, in May 1913. The suffragettes did many amazing things, they chained themselves to lamp-posts and to the railings outside No. 10 Downing Street, they suffered imprisonment for being disorderly and some sacrificed their lives.

No one told P.C. Langford what he was in for when he was detailed in the second week of May 1913 to attend a militant suffragette meeting in Pool Meadow, Coventry. When he arrived it looked as if it was going to be a rowdy meeting. His job was to guard the platform (a lorry drawn up against a wall), while a number of Police Officers were keeping an eye on the crowd. Soon after the women began their meeting, someone threw a paper bag filled with flour from over the wall of a nearby school (probably the Art School in Ford Street). It hit the Police Superintendent and burst all over his chest. Amid screams of laughter and cat calls, the man tried to make himself look a little less like a miller's man and more like a Police Officer. Something came flying towards P.C. Langford, he ducked, and an egg crashed against the wall behind him, dribbling down a bystander's neck. The meeting finally broke up in disorder, and with another officer, he went to the rescue of one of the suffragettes whom the crowd had captured. They rushed her to a nearly public house and guarded her in the Smoke Room, while the crowd lost sight of her. Some of the other suffragettes had been less fortunate and had to ride around the city in a tram to avoid violence.

Earlsdon Avenue near the library was the place for the suffragettes to hold their next meeting. After the Pool Meadow fracas P.C. Langford was told to keep a watch out for youths who used such meetings as an opportunity for hooliganism. These youths probably had not got a clue what the meeting was about, but simply arrived to cause trouble. On this occasion disorder

21

broke out quickly and stones were being thrown, as well as tomatoes, which hit a policeman's helmet. Two young men were summonsed for their part in all of this.

Meanwhile, the Police were busy with 'Operation Escort'. A plan had been devised for the controlling of the yobs by a high level of officers before the meeting. As soon as the meeting ended they were to get the suffragettes off the platform and down a jetty to Newcombe Road, where a hansom cab and detectives would be waiting. Unfortunately, the cab was late and after this everything happened. The crowd rushed round the back streets and started attacking the Police who were guarding the women. When the cab eventually arrived, the suffragettes scrambled in, the mob grabbed the cab's wheels and tried to tip it over. The Police beat them off and the women escaped.

The quiet that greeted the suffragettes at their next meeting, which was held at the corner of Lockhurst Lane, Foleshill, was merely the calm before a storm. Then uproar started when a man on an open-topped tram hurled a large piece of turf and it hit the speaker straight in the eye – a real 'bulls-eye'. In the middle of the disorder which followed, the Police rescued the suffragettes and took them to a nearby Trade Union Club; once in the club the Police were besieged. Whilst the crowds pushed and shoved outside the doors, the Police were attacked both as a body and individually. In the end it was the Police that won 'The battle of Lockhurst Lane', and the suffragettes were driven off in a four-wheeled cab with the mob shouting, 'You'd be better at home doing the washing up'.

One last incident marked the end of the campaign. The Fire Brigade one day received a call from a distant street alarm. The Brigade dashed through the streets, but instead of a fire they expected, there was a large placard which read 'Release Tom Mann' (he was a Coventry union man) and 'Give Women the Vote'. So you can see that the suffragettes had a rough time with members of the public.

In the Editorial of the *Coventry Graphic* dated 8th March 1913, it stated that local suffragettes persisted in making themselves a nuisance at the meeting of the ILP that evening. During Mr Roberts' address in the Baths Assembly Hall, Priory Street, Coventry, there was a lot of noise and heckling by the women and it was some time before an appeal for better manners prevailed. It was a well-known fact that in the past the ILP had appealed for stewards to 'man' the meetings of the WSPU and urged that in future they showed a greater presence at these women's meetings. Also in the Editorial dated 30th May 1913, the following was reported: 'The Police have had an unpleasant duty in protecting suffrage speakers in Coventry. There is no doubt that the fanatical and dangerous militant policy of the suffragists has aroused the anger of the public, and their speakers now need police protection or the results would be disastrous. Militancy begets militancy. The ordinary person is asking questions why ratepayers should be expected to provide a police force sufficient to cope with disorder brought about by those whom the attendance of the police is essential. The missiles used this week included eggs and a local journalist stopped one egg – every drop of it'.

In the *Coventry Graphic* of 1st February 1914, it was reported that militant suffragetism has spread to Coventry, for on Wednesday, immediately after twilight a destructive fluid was dropped into the letter box at the General Post Office, Hertford Street, Coventry and damage was done to at least two articles that had been posted. 'More than 50 letters, etc., were in the box at the time the attack was made'. The report went on to ask, who was this 'fanatical creature who could so demean herself (or himself) by resorting to this stupid act? It is not only stupid but inhuman…. No sane person will argue that aberrations of this kind are likely to advance the cause of Woman's Suffrage. The direct opposite is more likely to be the case.'

On the 13th March 1914 *Coventry Graphic* reported about a suffragette outrage. 'The suffragette interruptions at the Labour meeting at Coventry on Friday afford an example of how the more violent advocates of votes for women are setting back their own clock…. the Secretary of the Labour Party himself in seeking to speak at the Corn Exchange, was interrupted and forced into silence by the demonstrations of the suffragettes. Such tactics, emphasised by the deplorable defacing of the Rokeby Venus at the National Gallery this week are having the effect of alienating the sympathies of male supporters of women's suffrage, and where people could formerly be brought to discuss the subject they will not now even listen to it. The wild talk which has been indulged in by the suffragettes at Birmingham last week is the kind that brings despair to all who realise that the years of cumulative work for women's suffrage are being negatived by such methods. It is reasonable to suppose that if women were given the vote the present agitators would assume the leadership of the feminist movement and their present attitude and actions do not inspire confidence in their ability to undertake the role'.

In the archives at *Coventry History Centre*, the following letter is to be found under the heading 'Assertive female presumed to be a suffragette' dated 1913. It was sent to Mr Cecil Irby-Hopkins from Mrs Ethel S. Thackhall-Browett. The Thackhall-Browetts were tenants of Grove House, Keresley, just outside Coventry and obviously Mr Irby-Hopkins was the owner. She was complaining about the state of the garden and here is a brief outline of her letter: 'Have you ever seen this property of yours? It is becoming a wilderness. There are dozens of shrubs all being crowded out of existence and growing their heads off, and we are starting a new garden'. She goes on to write 'Couldn't you come down and see for yourself the hopelessly forlorn state the place is getting into. We have done our best at clearing this last year, but it is nothing but a home for friendless cats!' She then added a post-script, saying that she would be in town, next Tuesday until Friday at her Club – The Ladies Army and Navy Club, (I assume that she meant London) and suggested that he should call and see her. The Thackhall-Browetts turned out to be ailurophobes, (persons with an intense dislike or fear of cats).

Mr Irby-Hopkins responded by writing to his solicitor Mr G.H. Thynne on the 10th April 1913. He enclosed the letter that he had received from Mrs Thackhall-Browett and said 'I should think she must be a militant suffragette' and went on to write that he certainly did not intend to call on the woman. He also wrote that he had written to her to say that if she had any proposals to make that she should write directly to Mr Thynne and he would put the proposals before him in the usual way. He added 'I also told her that I could not stop things growing'.

The Thackhall-Browetts are buried in St. Mary's graveyard, Corley, near Coventry with the inscription on the headstone 'Rena in loving memory of Ethel Irene only daughter of William and Ethel S. Thackhall-Browett dated 8th June 1910 aged 27. Also her father who passed away 27th October 1933 aged 70 years and her mother who passed away 29th August 1942 aged 81 years'. The mother's death was registered in Eastbourne.

Suffragettes in Berkswell

It was not only city women but also country women who joined the suffragette movement. There was Lettice Annie Floyd of Berkswell, near Coventry (see our previous publication *Telling Tales*). Lettice was born in 1865, the daughter of William Floyd, gentleman and Alison Floyd (nee Clapperton). They were wealthy landowners and lived at Beechwood House, situated on the corner of Tanners Lane and Spencers Lane, Berkswell.

Lettice and her sister Mary set up a Berkswell Branch of the Birmingham and District Suffrage Society, but this was dissolved in 1908, when they left to join the WSPU. Lettice undertook speaking tours for this branch and became involved in many militant actions. She was a generous benefactor to the organisation. Lettice had family connections with the women's movement. Her mother was the sister of Jane Hume Clapperton who was an author and a member of the Edinburgh National Society for Women's Suffrage she also subscribed to the WSPU. Maybe it was Aunt Jane that influenced Lettice to join the movement.

It is interesting that the Floyd family were related to the Lant's who lived at Nailcote Hall, Berkswell and the Rotherhams, the watch manufacturers who lived at the Grange, Coundon, near Coventry. There were also many Rotherhams living in Berkswell who were mainly farmers and landowners.

Lettice and her sister Mary were friends of Maud Watson (1864-1946), who was the winner of the first ladies Lawn Tennis Championship at Wimbledon in 1884. Her father was the Rector of Berkswell.

In Trafalgar Square on the 11th October 1908 the public were invited to help the suffragettes 'rush' the House of Commons. Lettice took a full part in this action and served one month in prison, for wilfully obstructing police in the execution of their duty at Bridge Street, Westminster. Twenty-three women including Lettice, were sentenced to one month's imprisonment in Holloway Prison. She was released on the 21st November 1908.

The suffragette publication *Votes for Women* dated 29th October 1908 reporting from the Midlands, refers to Lettice Floyd, as 'our delegate', which suggests that she was in London in a representative capacity. The article went on to praise her for her 'courage and self-sacrifice', which would 'spur us onto renewed efforts'. Many of the suffragettes stayed at Beechwood House, Berkswell. I wonder if people in the village knew who

25

were these women?

The friendship between Lettice and Annie Williams probably began before October 1909. Annie was employed as a full time organiser of the WPSU for Newcastle-upon-Tyne and she remained there until the end of July 1911. Lettice left Berkswell to live with Annie and to act as her Literature Secretary. The friendship between these two women seems to be unusual, as Annie was born in Cornwall to an ordinary rural family, whereas Lettice was the daughter of a well to do family.

On the 6th January 1911 it was reported that Annie Williams was speaking in Coventry and this had been arranged by Miss Helen Dawson of St. Peter's Vicarage, Hillfields. In March 1912 Annie and Lettice became involved in a window-smashing campaign in London. The mass window-smashing began on Friday 1st March in the West End and there were further attacks in the following days.

According to the *Women's Who's Who*, Lettice was arrested on the 4th March 1913 for breaking a window; that evening there were 96 arrests. Targets were Black Rod's office at the House of Lords, The Lord Chancellor's residence in Eaton Square, Central Post Offices, Lord Cromer's house and the Knightsbridge area. Annie and Lettice were arrested and both sent to Holloway Prison, Annie for one month and Lettice for two months hard labour for 'wilful damage'. Lettice took part in a hunger-strike in prison in support of suffragette prisoners in Aylesbury Prison. She was released from prison on the 2nd May 1912. Around this time her sister Mary gave ten shillings towards a fund to raise money for food hampers for suffragette prisoners.

In November 1912 both Lettice and her sister Mary contributed to George Lansbury's expenses when he stood as a suffrage candidate. Lansbury was a Labour MP who had resigned his seat in protest at Government policy regarding the suffragettes. Unfortunately, he failed to retain his seat at the by-election.

Lettice was still the 'Literature Secretary' and was occupied with propaganda work for *The*

Lettice Floyd.

Suffragette newspaper and she was kept busy selling it.

At the start of the 1914-1918 war, one of the Floyd sisters served on the committee of the War Savings Club, which was established in 1916. Lettice's friend Maud Watson was very active as she was Commandant of the Berkswell Rectory Auxiliary Hospital (VAD), at Well House, Berkswell. It is possible that Lettice, ran the first local Workers Educational Association course, held at the rear of the Wesleyan Chapel, Berkswell. It ran for twenty sessions from October 1915 - March 1916. Towards the end of the war Mary, who was Lettice's older sister died aged 58. She had been suffering from depression and killed herself by taking poison. At this time she was living at 'Hillside', Station Road, Balsall Common.

In 1920 a Berkswell Branch of the Women's Institute was founded on an initiative by Maud Watson, Lettice Floyd and Annie Williams along with other local women.

Lettice Floyd died on the 4th April 1934 aged 68 in Bushwood Nursing Home, Edgbaston, in Birmingham. Annie Williams was present at her death. Lettice is buried in the Floyd family vault in the graveyard at Berkswell.

Looking back in time many people were not in favour of militancy but what else could be done to get their point across when the government would not listen to them.

For those of you who are Family Historians, many suffragettes refused to fill in the form for the 1911 census. In which case refusal was noted on the records, or they stayed away from home for the whole night of the census thereby evading being counted at all. It is not known exactly how many boycotted the census in this way, but it could be up to several thousand.

We have a lot to thank these brave women for. Without them we would not have equal rights of the vote with the men. Therefore we should always use our vote no matter what we think.

VOTES FOR WOMEN

Angela Atkin

Acknowledgements

Thank you to Coventry History Centre for their help.
Thank you to Connie Fell of Berkswell Local History Group.
Thank you to Alan Tucker for his help and for permission to use the photograph of Lettice Floyd.

Bibliography

The title was inspired by *Alice Hawkins and the Suffragette Movement in Edwardian Leicester* – Dr Richard Whitmore
The Women's Suffrage Movement in Britain and Ireland – Elizabeth Crawford
Suffragette Partnership Lettice Floyd and Annie Williams – Alan Tucker
Newspaper Cuttings for the *Coventry Graphic* March 1914 February 1914 and March 1914.
Midland Daily Telegraph February 1939
Coventry Herald 1939
Coventry Standard 1951

Canary Girls
Munitions Workers in the First World War

The First World War was the first experience of 'Total War' in Europe and other countries around the world. The term 'Total War' was coined to describe the involvements of all aspects of life, for those countries taking part, in the conflict. Civilians were not divorced from the fighting, but had to contribute in a way never envisaged before.

When war was declared on 4th August 1914 men volunteered to join the armed forces, full of patriotism and believing that it would all be over by Christmas. Men were encouraged to play their part through campaigns in the press and verbal questioning of their courage. As the war escalated so the factories making armaments and munitions found they needed more staff to increase production. In 1915 that shortage was taken up enthusiastically by women.

The government had taken over chemical works in London and set up others at Oldbury, Queensferry and Gretna in the early months of the war to make explosives like tri-nitro toluene (TNT), cordite, gun cotton and others. By the end of the war there were 32 government factories manufacturing explosives. Engineering factories and vehicle manufacturers turned their production towards the war effort by making shells, military vehicles, aircraft and later tanks. As Coventry was the centre of the car industry, many of those factories went over to war work immediately. Rover, Daimler, Rudge Whitworth and Standard all went over to munitions production. The Ordnance works near Red Lane was established in 1905 and White and Poppe, an engineering factory in Lockhurst Lane, superseded all others by becoming the largest producer of munitions in the city by the end of the war. Siddeley Deasy manufactured aircraft, the Standard Company also made aircraft from 1915 and Alfred Herbert's made machine tools.

The Cabinet Committee meeting on 23rd December 1914 talked of expanding the system of 'dilution' of available labour. Dilution was a rather derogatory term for using women in traditional male jobs. On 16th March the first systematic attempt to enrol women for replacement of male labour was made by the Board of Trade. By the beginning of June 1915, 18,946 women were enrolled on a special War Register for work in munitions, but only 1,816 had actually been found a job. It was obvious that women were willing and able to work in factories, but there was a reluctance to employ them. Lloyd George called women's war work a 'revolution' put into effect by the war.

It was believed that women would dilute the skills normally associated with engineering jobs. Naturally the unions were not in favour of women doing men's jobs because they thought it would undermine their status and privilege within the workforce. Women were traditionally paid only about half the rate of a man and the unions did not want to encourage the employers to replace their men with unskilled men, boys or women. The Amalgamated Society of Engineers (ASE) negotiated with the government over the conditions under which they would agree to dilution. The unions wanted there to be equal pay to prevent their rates being undermined. They extracted a promise from the government that all concessions that they had agreed to would be rewarded at the end of hostilities by dismissing all dilutees.

Despite the union eventually agreeing to a compromise it did not mean that the employers would abide by the agreement. In many cases they did just what the unions feared and used women as cheap labour. Although there were Munitions Tribunals, where women could appeal if their wages were too low, their cases were not always dealt with sympathetically. Women were also tied to one factory once they agreed to work there. They needed a leaving certificate if they wanted to move to another factory with better rates of pay. However, their current employer could refuse to give them a leaving certificate. It caused a great deal of friction, but the woman was powerless if the Tribunal did not support her.

All the fears of men that women could not perform the tasks they were allotted were proved groundless. With a little flexibility, women usually learned on the job, watching a skilled worker, or were sent away for a period of training, generally a couple of weeks. Tasks were made easier for women by a simple adaptation of working conditions to suit the generally smaller stature of women, such as benches lowered or duckboards to raise them up to the correct height. Equipment and tools could be made smaller and lighter to facilitate a more efficient workplace. The war created the opportunity to improve conditions in factories by using female labour on a large scale.

It was realised by government that women could not be expected to put up with the sort of primitive conditions that men had endured before the war. From August 1915 women staff inspectors were employed to check on munitions factories to make sure that standards were maintained. Her duties included giving advice and help in the selection of women supervisors of labour. Doctors were appointed to oversee the welfare of the workers in large establishments.

Lloyd George appointed a Health of Munitions Workers Committee in September 1915 to advise on the question of 'industrial fatigue, hours of labour and matters affecting health and physical efficiency' of munitions workers. Those workers spent long hours in crowded conditions and needed provision of lavatories, cloakrooms, canteens and mess rooms. These were easier to ensure in government controlled, newly built factories, but not so easy to monitor in smaller, private and older establishments. The government wanted to re-educate employers into providing greater welfare rather than compelling them. Such items as overalls and caps to protect girls from being contaminated by noxious substances, that they came into contact with during their working hours, were provided as the norm as the war progressed.

A munitions worker assembling shells.

Girls working on munitions were the most vulnerable to health problems due to the chemicals used in the composition of explosives. Amongst the varied chemicals used to fill the shells were cordite, which gave some girls headaches, caused hysteria and sometimes fits, especially if there was a tendency towards epilepsy. As it had a sweet taste, some girls were tempted to eat it, but it made them very sick indeed. Some girls were affected by the fumes given off by the chemicals, which could cause fainting and fits. TNT that was widely used during the war caused toxic jaundice, turning the skin yellow and the hair a green or ginger shade. It did cause a number of deaths. Compound Explosive (CE) was not lethal, but caused sickness, discolouration of the skin and dermatitis. It is no wonder that girls working with these chemicals became known as canary girls. If the jaundice was bad they were taken off the work and put on to other work before it developed into a serious health problem. The girls often went back to their original job after they recovered.

It was not just in the munitions factories where chemicals were used. The 'dope' used to coat the surface of fabric-covered planes, to tighten, waterproof and varnish it, was also poisonous. Ventilation was not always adequate in such workshops and there was very little attention paid to using masks. A small number of deaths occurred due to the use of 'dope,' although it caused fainting, sickness and headaches. Deaths and accidents did not just occur in munitions factories, but in heavy industries and manufacturers of engines and vehicles, where the workplace was hazardous and caution was necessary at all times. Before health and safety legislation, machines were not protected with guards and fingers, hair and clothing could be caught up.

Coventry Munitions

Gertrude Sellors accompanied her husband when he was called up to work in a munitions factory in Coventry during the First World War. Initially their daughter was with them, but she returned to relatives in Yorkshire to complete her education. Accommodation was hard to find as the influx of workers to Coventry put pressure on the limited housing stock. They found a bedroom to rent in Stoney Stanton Road for two weeks, moved to rooms in Station Street and then found a house to rent in Eld Road.

Her husband worked at a munitions factory in Holbrooks Lane, which must have been White and Poppe, whose new factory covered an extensive site in Holbrooks Lane (later it became the Dunlop factory). Gertrude also found herself a position there testing fuses. She remarked that the screw in the fuse had to be fitted very tightly. If she could get them tight, she could proceed to pack them up. She became mistress of a corridor, overseeing a number of girls in her section. At the end of the day a train took the completed munitions to a place near Leeds and returned each night for more. A branch line of the railway came right into the factory for ease of loading and security.

Many of the girls under her supervision lived in the hostels built around the periphery of the factory to accommodate the workers. Blocks of huts housed 100 girls to a hut, under the control of a matron. By 1916 there were 32 huts of very basic construction, which were improved over time. Colony Cottages were built on the opposite side of Holbrooks Lane to the factory. Holbrook Lane Cottages were on the south side of the site and Whitmore Park Cottages to the north on the other side of Foleshill Park. Alongside the hostels were extensive allotments, which were used to grow vegetables and fruit for the canteen at the factory.

When Gertrude Sellors heard from her sister that her house in Yorkshire had been badly damaged, she wanted to resign and rush back to her home. However, the management would not let her leave, but gave her a week's compassionate leave to sort things out, with the promise of a munitions cottage when she returned. She described Holbrooks as very rural at the time, but it gradually became an estate for the workers. She says that the bungalows and cottages were very nice and she and her husband lived there for some years after the war. The cottages were built in rows, with about 20-24 in each row. Munitions Cottages were the first to be built but deteriorated in the end and were demolished. Colony Cottages had three to four bedrooms and lasted longer. They were council owned, but they too deteriorated over the years. They were only built as temporary residences and never meant to last as long as they did.

Within the factory were six large units. Girls worked on tapping jigs, thread mills, capstans, automatic machines, presses and other machinery. There were tool rooms in each factory, with the setting done by men. Later women took over these jobs too. Filling fuses was done in a separate factory on the site. It was known as National Factory No.21. Ten women were sent for training at Woolwich and they became the forewomen who trained the girls on the job.

Girls came from all over the country to work on munitions. To distinguish where they had come from they had a separate colour. English was red, Scottish was blue, and Irish green. They did not mark Welsh girls as a separate unit, but perhaps they should have been yellow for daffodils. By the end of 1916, 4,000 women and 800 men were working in the filling factory alone. The explosives were stored underground for safety reasons. Over the period of the First World War White and Poppe employed over 30,000 people and became one of the largest in the country.

There was not just work going on at the factory, but leisure activities for the employees too. There were sports rooms with associated teams, a swimming pool, a library, a recreation hall and canteen. When the London theatres closed down, some of the actors came to live in Colony Cottages. They put on shows and operettas by Gilbert and Sullivan. Gertrude Sellors saw *HMS Pinafore* and *The Gondoliers* there. Lillian Miles and her sister came from Exeter to work at White and Poppe and later at the Ordnance. She was very fond of opera and frequently attended the Opera House in Hales Street. If you did not like sports and entertainment, there were always the allotments to be worked on. There were also Scout and Girl Guide troops to belong to, with associated activities.

The whole factory site was guarded by soldiers who were accommodated in barracks opposite the munitions works. At the time of Gertrude Sellors' interview in August 1968, when she was 88 years old, her home was the original Officers Mess at the factory.

At White and Poppe they were fortunate that accommodation was available to house the workforce, in fact they had over-capacity. At other factories workers were not catered for in the same way. The first housing scheme in Coventry during the war was carried out in the Stoke Heath area of the city for workers at the Ordnance works. Accommodation was scarce in Coventry and in great demand. When Lillian Miles and her sister came to the city to work they found accommodation very hard to find. Lillian recalled that beds were being used in shifts called 'box and cox,' as one girl got out to go to work another got in after her shift at the factory. The first place that she and her sister stayed was filthy and they were soon looking for an alternative. She did not seem to have a high opinion of the Irish girls, whom she said, did not seem to mind slumming it with six to a bed. She and her sister eventually found better lodgings with the foreman's family.

Members of the Advisory Committee on Women's War Employment (Industrial) looked at accommodation in Coventry in 1916. They found that houses condemned and closed by the Corporation, were reopened to house workers after some refurbishment. Rising prices and scarcity inflated the cost of accommodation too. Often a high proportion of their wages were spent on paying for a roof over their heads. No wonder these girls were willing to go into purpose-built hostels at the factories.

When the war came to an end, production of munitions came to an end. The mass of women workers who had covered the jobs of men who went off to fight in the war, were summarily dismissed. As the unions had demanded when they agreed to women doing men's jobs, the women had to go. Women were unwilling to go back to poorly paid domestic jobs after the war. They had been used to earning better wages than ever before and did not want to return to the life of drudgery they had experienced prior to the war.

In an article by Mrs Givens entitled *Coventry and the Unemployed* published in the *Woman Worker* in February 1919 it stated that 3,500 women were on Donation Benefit in Coventry. She and Alice Arnold of the Workers Union spoke at a meeting of unemployed women. She stated that only 5% of women were willing to take up domestic service, living in, if conditions and wages improved and 30% if living out. However, 65% would not take such work at all. Some unemployed women lost benefit by refusing domestic work. Mrs Givens wanted government to provide retraining for other skills, as employers were unwilling to do so.

Women over the age of 30 and with a property qualification were entitled to vote in general elections in 1918, in recognition of the work they had done towards the war effort. However, they still had a struggle to find work after the war when the men who survived the trenches returned to their pre-war jobs. Women did gain some independence and proved that they were capable of holding down jobs not considered suitable for them. Life would never be quite the same again.

Lynn Hockton

Acknowledgements

Recording of an interview with Gertrude Sellors, *Life and conditions in Coventry munitions work* by Dr Kenneth Richardson. Richardson Tape Collection, Media Services, Lanchester Library, Coventry University.

Bibliography

White & Poppe Ltd: Engine Manufacturers, Coventry – Jeromy Hassell
Women Munitions Workers in Coventry During the First World War – Claire Beasley
On Her Their Lives Depend: Munitions Workers in the Great War – Angela Woollacott
War Memoirs of David Lloyd George
The Virago Book of Women and the Great War – Edited by Joyce Marlow

'We are going strong - like the tanks'[1] : Coventry women workers and trade unions in the First World War

Rumours and myths about women munitions workers in Britain abounded during the First World War. When in 1917 Mary Macarthur, the secretary of the National Federation of Women Workers (the Federation), spoke of her union's demand for a two pence pay increase for women, she referred to 'the exaggerated statements which frequently appeared in the British press as to the inflated earnings of women munitions workers'. 'Some of these scribblers,' it was noted, seem to think that 'our exclusive diet was expensive chocolate creams and our chief attire sealskin coats'.[2] Women, it was suggested, were already being paid more than they knew what to do with and were frittering away their wages on 'fancy' items that were firmly judged to be well out of the league of working class 'girls'. The workers themselves and those who sought to organise them into trade unions knew that the reality was very different. Wages did increase from their pre-war levels, particularly for women who moved into munitions' production from the so-called 'women's trades', including clothing production, laundry work and domestic service. The trade unions that enrolled women, however, kept up constant pressure on both government and employers, seeking to ensure that pay agreements were adhered to and that women received the pay rates and working arrangements that they had been promised. In 1917, after hearing an employer expressing concern about the grave moral danger of young women earning too much money, Macarthur's perceptive observation was that she had never heard an employer either before or during the War express concern about the moral dangers of *low* wages. '[Macarthur] could not say,' it was reported, 'that such an argument left her cold, because it plunged her into a fever heat of indignation'.[3]

Munitions work was physically dangerous; in 1916 the Midland Daily Telegraph reported that in Coventry Miss Winifred Chattaway had been operating a drilling machine 'when her hair became tangled with the drill, causing severe head injuries'.[4] Florence Jackson, who worked at the Coventry Ordnance Fuse Factory in Red Lane, recalled the dangers associated with the work there:

'They used to fill the shell bodies with powder, and often one blew up… occasionally you'd get a spark off and it will go… My stepmother worked there. One of her friends, they said had her face blown to bits'.[5]

Another worker at the Ordnance, Isabel Magee (who married after the War, becoming Mrs Clark), had come to England from Belfast when she was just fifteen. Along with a friend, she was sent by the Labour Exchange to a munitions factory in Morecambe where the girls were employed to fill shells with gas powder. Involvement in this dangerous and highly secretive work poisoned and killed her young friend. Recalling that 'I never got over it, her dying', Isabel returned to Belfast before being redirected to the Ordnance in Coventry some months later, joining women from England, Scotland and Ireland, living in hostel accommodation in Swan Lane.[6]

In addition to the danger, hours in factories that produced war materials could be excessively long and despite pay increases, the cost of living during the War soared, with food prices and other essentials such as heating, lighting, rent, clothes and travel rising substantially.[7] Many women struggled to make ends meet. One young mother wrote to the Federation's paper, *The Woman Worker* in 1917 to complain that 'it is almost impossible to live on the money owing to the terrible increase in prices of food'. Her earnings, for producing soldiers' mess tins, were just 12 and a half shillings for a 52 and a half hour week, with a two shillings war bonus which was stopped if she was late. Her outgoings were 'three shillings a week for my baby to be taken care of during my absence (she was rushing home in her midday break to feed her child), two shillings a week for rent, one shilling for washing, three pence health insurance and two and a half pence unemployment insurance'. The remains of her money went on food, fuel and light. 'And as regards asking for a rise, it is out of the question'.[8] A letter to the socialist paper, *The Woman's Dreadnought*, highlights some of the difficulties faced by wives of soldiers and sailors who, despite receiving separation allowances, did not have enough to live on:

'I have four children and have to earn 2 or 3 shillings extra to be able to live. The cheapest meat is 1s 2d or 1s 3d per pound and we can hardly look at that. Here are my accounts. Army pay 34s 6d; 6s rent, 6s bread, 3s insurance, 2s coals, 2s margarine, 1s 6d jam, 3s to keep them in boots, 1s 4d tea, 6d coffee, 2s milk, 1s light[ing]…that leaves 6s for me to get for myself and four children dinners for seven days and sugar (that we scarcely see), soap, wood, soda and other useful things. It is killing us women to know how to go on day after day'.[9]

This is a study of how trade unions in wartime Coventry worked to introduce women workers to the benefits of membership. They sought not just to relieve them of their weekly subscription fees but to be of help as so many adjusted to a new way of life, travelling distances to work, some in digs or hostels away from home, others coping as single parents with their husbands away at the Front. The unions believed that given the opportunity, employers would, as they had always done, seek to employ women as cheap labour. The case of the young mother on twelve shillings a week in 1917 suggests that such fears were justified and that women needed the protection of the union. Women workers themselves gained confidence as union members, supported one another and heeded organisers' calls to encourage their colleagues to join. They discovered that there was companionship and fun in their local branch, with regular dances and socials that combined entertainment with education in union life. They also embraced the more serious side of union life, many taking on active roles in the factories as shop stewards and 'subs' collectors, and secretaries and treasurers within the branch. Some women became so adept at and absorbed in their roles that they became paid union officials, as was the case for two Coventry women, Henrietta Givens and Alice Arnold. Whilst few women trade unionists' voices have been preserved by history, those that have been recorded allow us to learn something of women's experiences of work in Coventry, the city that, on account of its factories, often gave the impression of being 'the busiest place in England' during the First World War.[10] We should be, however, wary of forming the impression that a conviction in the importance of trade unionism was shared by all women workers. Despite a 160% national increase in the number of women trade unionists during the First World War,[11] not all women workers joined a union and others, even as members, were indifferent to or unconvinced of its significance. For example, Elsie Farlow, who worked at the Ordnance in Red Lane, could not remember either joining a union or paying 'subs', nor could she recall any trade union activity at the factory.[12] Such experiences, however, stood in sharp contrast to those who discovered deeply rewarding work through their involvement in wartime trade unionism, such as Alice Arnold, who later declared that 'her heart and soul were with the labour movement'.[13]

In 1916 the local press was referring to the arrival of thousands of women workers from all over Britain and Ireland to work in Coventry's many munitions' factories. Nationally the number of women employed in industry increased by nearly 800,000 between July 1914 and July 1918 and with the expansion of war production from 1916, a large proportion of these workers went into munitions.[14] Despite the fact that women were not entering the factories for the first time, they were certainly more visible than they had been before the War, moving in larger numbers than previously, into the types of industrial roles that were traditionally regarded as 'men's work' and, as we have seen, attracting press attention. Lynn Hockton's article notes the initial moral panic that ensued as women, both as dilutees and as direct substitutes, entered the engineering industries. Some unions, catering for unskilled and semi-skilled workers, had opened their doors to women before the War and the sheer numbers of women moving into munitions as the War progressed forced others to act. The exclusively male Amalgamated Society of Engineers (ASE) came to believe that if male wage levels were to be maintained and protected after the War, something ought to be done to organise women. This was often regarded as a necessity to deal with the perceived 'menace' of low paid women workers rather than being offered in a spirit of comradeship and encouragement to women to join their brothers in the labour movement. In Coventry, their members' nervousness was apparent early on in the War, with men reporting back to the union when they learned of girls being 'started' at engineering firms. For example, in June 1915, four union brothers informed the ASE that women newly appointed to work on shells and fuses at the Rudge Whitworth Cycle Factory were, at 2 ½ pence an hour, displacing men at 6 ½ pence from another department.[15] Continued anxiety led the union to work with the Coventry branch of the women's Federation and this will be looked at in more detail a little later.

Questions of women's pay began to be addressed by the Ministry of Munitions in 1915 and by early 1916 it was agreed that women in both government owned and controlled munitions factories employed on 'men's work' should be paid a pound for a 48 hour week.[16] Obtaining such rates, however, was seldom straightforward and the case of Isabel Magee at the Ordnance serves as a good example of the difficulties women encountered in obtaining anything like equal pay with men. Often men were employed to set up the machines that women workers operated and so, by ensuring that the work that men and women were doing could not be regarded as the same, pay differentials could be maintained. When Isabel Magee was taught by a helpful male inspector how to set up her own machine, it was Alice Arnold of the Workers' Union (WU) who helped to make sure that, as the first to be allowed to do this, she was paid the right rate for the job. Even so, this was not instantly forthcoming; despite her skill, she was told by a government official that she was still not entitled to be paid the men's rate because she was not grinding her own tools. Once she had been taught to do this she found that she was *still* not earning what she had been told to expect, this time because she was not old enough. With so many barriers, a young woman worker needed not just the help of a sympathetic male colleague but a committed trade union official who could provide her with all the necessary information to achieve a fair wage. Isabel Magee remembered Alice Arnold as 'a wonderful person for working women... it was her really, she fought for the rate' and her efforts were successful.[17]

The majority of women who joined trade unions during the War became members of the general unions catering for unskilled and semi skilled workers. In Coventry two important unions catering for women workers were the WU and the Federation. The key difference between the two was that whilst the WU had a mixed sex membership, the Federation was for women only. They had competed for members during disputes in Coventry before the War and the WU, believing strongly that men and women should be organised together, was critical of the Federation for its single sex approach to membership, implying that it was misguided in placing the interests of sex before class. In fact, the long term view of the Federation was that women *were* better served in unions which admitted men and women but its leadership judged that whilst so many unions still refused to open their doors to women, the Federation was necessary until women were welcome members of all trade unions.

Both unions sought to recruit members from among women munitions workers in the Coventry factories. The WU relied on its chief women's officer, Julia Varley, and the women's organiser for Birmingham, Emily Weaver, to generate enthusiasm in Coventry. Varley recorded in 1916 that the city was 'forging ahead in a magnificent manner and the men members taking up the question of the women's organisation in the most energetic way, while membership is going up by leaps and bounds'.[18] Social events were a good way of bringing large numbers of women together and in 1916 she reported on the success of a dance at one of the works, despite the distinct lack of male dancing partners for the women. She noted that, 'owing to a large number of the "best boys" being at the Front, the pretty sex predominated. I was much struck with the appearance of the girls while dancing, and owing to the absence of the sombre attire of mere man, the effect was very dainty, most of the girls being in light colours'.[19]

In addition to Varley and Weaver, the Coventry based WU organiser, George Morris, was working hard to protect the interests of women workers. At a Munitions Tribunal in 1917 he protested 'against the disgraceful ways in which girls were brought to Coventry on promises of wages far in excess of what they actually received'. The case that he was involved in illustrates the need women had of trade union protection against employers who still, even during the War, tended to exploit women as cheap labour whenever they spotted an opportunity to do so. Morris was defending a young woman called Annie Whitfield, living at Whitmore Park Hostels and who had been dismissed from her work without notice. She had been recruited at the Aberdeen Labour Exchange and sent to Coventry, where she was informed that two shillings a week would be deducted from her wages until her rail fare from Scotland had been paid for, but that this would later be refunded. The deduction, however, amounted to seven shillings a week for four weeks and in addition, her wages were being paid at a much lower rate than the one she had been led to expect. Miss Whitfield claimed that whilst it had been agreed that she would earn six pence an hour plus a bonus, she was in fact only receiving half of this rate. She was also bullied by the charge hand and dismissed for refusing to work, despite the fact that she could not do her job because her machine was defective. The Tribunal Chairman gave judgement for a week's wages to be paid to Miss Whitfield and the case was adjourned so that the proper rate for the job could be determined. George Morris declared that girls were being brought to Coventry under false pretences; Annie Whitfield, he said, had left 'a good position in Aberdeen, earning not less than £2 2s a week on the promises made and on the title of this Coventry factory she gave up that situation' to come to the city.[20]

In the autumn of 1917 the WU decided to appoint a full time women's organiser in Coventry. Its choice, Alice Arnold, was a Coventry born woman who worked at Rudge Whitworth, a cycle factory turned government controlled munitions plant. As a shop steward for the WU, Arnold had proved her worth as a valuable union official, working to recruit hundreds of women workers as union members.[21] She was exactly the sort of appointment the WU liked - a down to earth working class woman with a long history of factory employment; by 1917, although only 36, she had worked in Coventry factories for up to 25 years and had been a union member for at least 12.[22] Margaret Jeffs, who became an inspector of machine parts at the Deasy on Parkside, recorded her respect for Alice Arnold who, as 'an old pioneer' was a regular factory gate speaker, delivering 'really down to earth speeches...

because she'd lived in one of the poorest parts of the city'. The implication was that Arnold understood the needs of working women and was, as Isabel Magee had also recognised, ready to work to defend them.[23]

In November 1917, Alice Arnold reported that around 200 women were joining the WU in Coventry

Workers at Siddeley Deasy

every month. Her enthusiasm was apparent in her belief that 'we are going strong - like the tanks' and that, as membership went up by 'leaps and bounds... the women are getting as strong as the men'.[24] Progress was good despite the fact that 'competition with another organisation' had been noted in the city in 1916.[25] The competition, with the Federation, was at times fierce, causing division within the local labour movement. Nationally the Federation worked in alliance during the War with the ASE, the engineers' union, which, although it would not accept women into its own ranks, decided to help the Federation to recruit women. It was motivated by its recognition of the dangers to be faced from unorganised women workers but also partly by a desire to prevent general unions such as the WU from becoming too powerful. In return for the ASE's help, the Federation agreed to withdraw its members from the skilled men's jobs at the end of the War to allow pre-war labour conditions to resume. In Coventry the alliance between the ASE and the Federation was closer than in many munitions centres and was managed by a husband and wife team. Walter Givens was District Secretary of the ASE and his wife, Henrietta, became the Federation's Coventry organiser in 1917, having previously been a prominent branch official. Henrietta Givens was born in Leeds and came to Coventry in 1897, where she was an early and active member of the city's branch of the Independent Labour Party and stood unsuccessfully for election as a Poor Law Guardian. After the War, she had the honour of becoming Coventry's first woman magistrate in 1920 and was elected as a Labour councillor in 1933. The wartime work of the Givens' partnership received the grateful help of the Federation's national leadership – 'our indefatigable friends' - as it uncovered numerous cases of injustice and securing pay awards for its members.[26] Whilst Walter Givens was tireless in his efforts to assist the Federation, it would seem that not all local ASE members were so willing to help women workers; May Ford, a Federation shop steward, remembered that it took a long time for the men to recognise the women as trade unionists. The Federation was 'allowed' to meet at the ASE premises and in time the men did admit the women to their Saturday afternoon meetings but, recalled Ford, 'not with open arms. We were never very welcome'.[27]

The Federation's work was just as intense and demanding as the WU's. Whenever possible, the Federation exposed poor working conditions and secured wage levels for women munitions workers. In January 1917, for example, the Coventry branch reported unsatisfactory wage levels at White and Poppe's munitions factory, where, in addition, it noted that the canteens were 'uncomfortable' and where several cases of eczema from working with tetryl had been reported.[28] In March 1917, piece rates were, thanks to its efforts, to be restored to the men's rates 'and the rate fixer has been dismissed'.[29] In March 1918 the Federation discovered that a young woman, Miss Campbell, was doing the work of a fully skilled man and had been awarded his rate without deductions. The employers and the Ministry of Munitions, however, had 'nibbled' at this rate and 'have decided that the fully skilled man's rate means his rate of last March plus the women's increases since then and does not mean - as it should - his rate, including all war increases'.[30] Here, then, was another example of an attempt to ensure that a pay differential between men and women existed even when women were doing exactly the same work as men. The Federation was determined to ensure that such injustices were eradicated.

Social events were as important to the Federation as they were to the WU. Although the evening of Saturday November 4th 1916 turned out to be very wet, the union journal, *The Woman Worker*, noted that it 'did not keep the girls away' from a dance at the Coventry Co-operative Assembly Rooms in West Orchard. 'It was a jolly set of girls that rallied together and everyone seemed to be bent on having a good time; at seven thirty the dancing was in full swing'. During the interval, the Federation's Organising Secretary, Margaret Bondfield (future Labour MP and Britain's first woman Cabinet minister) addressed the girls and 'a very pleasant and happy evening closed at 10.45 with a very strong desire among the girls that a similar social should take place'.[31]

By the end of the War the WU and the Federation both had around 80,000 women members across Britain.[32] It is likely that the decision of which union to join depended to a large extent on which was encountered first and on which was most active either inside the factory or at the factory gate. Coventry worker Margaret Jeffs explained that she believed it was 'the proper thing to be in a union', a view that she kept for the rest of her life.[33] Before the War, women had often been the victims of employers determined to keep the unions out of the workplace. When employed in small factories, workshops or as sweated home workers, they could be easily intimidated into giving up or resisting union membership, threatened with dismissal or bullied by foremen and women. For example, in 1907 the Women's Trade Union League was holding an outdoor meeting for women workers in Coventry when someone spotted the local employer walking by. The women, anxious that they would be recognised, fled the scene.[34] In contrast, employed in much larger departments during the War, women were more able to recognise the benefits of union membership and, as significantly, they could more easily afford to pay their subscriptions, whereas before the War casual work and extremely low pay had often made this difficult.

At the end of the War as women left the munitions factories, the unions fought hard to retain their membership, hoping that the experience of being in a union would, for all women workers, have become what the WU referred to as a life 'habit'.[35] Many women, however, disappeared back into a world of traditional, hidden and low paid 'women's work', forced by post war unemployment back into domestic service, laundry work and industrial work in which they were once again vulnerable to victimisation. During the 1920s and 30s, women organisers within the unions faced ever greater challenges, particularly when confronted with the problems of high unemployment.

Cathy Hunt

[1] Alice Arnold, Workers' Union *Record*, February 1918

[2] *The Woman Worker*, May 1917

[3] *The Woman Worker*, August 1917

[4] *Midland Daily Telegraph* January 13th 1916

[5] *Red Lane Reminiscences* (1983) , Red Lane Old Residents Association

[6] Red Lane Oral History Project, Coventry Archives

[7] A Woolacott (1994) *On Her Their Lives Depend: Munitions Workers in the Great War*, University of California Press, p118

[8] *The Woman Worker*, May 1917

[9] *The Woman's Dreadnought*, June 30th 1917

[10] J Yates (1950) *Pioneers to Power*, Coventry Labour Party, p 56

[11] S Boston (1987) *Women Workers and Trade Unions*, Lawrence & Wishart, p 126

[12] Imperial War Museum Sound Archive 773/1

[13] *Midland Daily Telegraph*, 27 April 1931

[14] Woolacott, *On Her Their Lives Depend*, p18

[15] June 18th 1915, Amalgamated Society of Engineers Minute Books, Coventry Archives

[16] D Thom (2000) *Nice Girls and Rude Girls: Women Workers in World War One*, IB Tauris, p60

[17] Red Lane Oral History Project

[18] Workers' Union *Record*, August 1916

[19] Workers' Union *Record*, May 1916

[20] Workers' Union *Record*, October 1917

[21] Letter from Billy Buxton to K Roberts, November 1965, Coventry Archives

[22] C Hunt (2008), *A Woman of the People: Alice Arnold of Coventry 1881-1955*, Coventry

Historical Association

[23] Imperial War Museum Sound Archive 826/2

[24] Workers' Union *Record*, November 1917; February 1918

[25] Workers' Union *Record*, June 1916

[26] *The Woman Worker*, March 1918

[27] Richardson Tape Collection, Media Services, Coventry (Lanchester) University Library, May Ford, December 1973

[28] *The Woman Worker*, January 1917

[29] *The Woman Worker*, March 1917

[30] *The Woman Worker*, March 1918

[31] *The Woman Worker*, December 1916

[32] B Drake (1920) *Women in Trade Unions*, Table 2 (Virago, 1984)

[33] Imperial War Museum Sound Archive, 826/2

[34] *Women's Trade Union Review*, October 1907

[35] Workers' Union *Record*, August 1916

Acknowledgements

Thank you to David Fry for permission to use the picture of the Siddeley Deasy women workers.

The Legacy of Hillcrest

It was 1946, at the top of Bishop Street the traffic was kept flowing by the regular policeman, swiftly directing from his podium wearing long white cuffs, like a tick-tack man with inside knowledge. Tom and Gwen meet again, on the crowded pavement - he very proud of his small son, in tow, she with a charming dark haired little three year old girl, Lorraine, plus a baby in the pram - me. Their shared past had been in the Coventry Children's homes before the war. They reminisced a little, and then Tom held his son up to look in the pram at the baby. Little did they know that the little boy and baby girl would provide their grandchildren, in the future, (reader I married him!) or that Gwen, only 22, would be dead within the year.

Tom (my father-in-law) had been in Hillcrest, Coventry Council's boys' home. He knew he had been in the way at home, and would go on at 14 years old to be placed by Coventry Homes in one of the training ships on the Thames in London, a sort of approved school with a very harsh regime. He stayed bitterly angry about this all his life, feeling the injustice keenly, as his only crime was being unwanted by his mother. By contrast he loved, and was loved by his grandmother; her occupation on her death certificate was 'bird scarer' at Berkswell.

The large boys' home was on Radford Road, between Barr's Hill girls' school, and a private house. At the back of it was Naul's Mill, (by then a park) built as a water mill in the 12th Century and in the distant past it had milled the Fullers Earth that arrived from Cornwall and used by weavers to give cloth body. In Tom's time it was a pleasant park, as it is now.

Hillcrest was quite a large building, the boys slept in individual beds in a large dormitory upstairs. The dining room, wash room, playroom, and study were very spacious and not what most of the children had been used to. Matron's room was on the ground floor. It was also said to be haunted. Tom was not happy there, and spent a lot of time mulling over his mother's rejection of him. This turned into a chip on his shoulder in later life. The policy at Hillcrest seems to have been tough but fair.

He told me that they would be given a present by the Corporation on Christmas morning. *The Coventry Standard* would come along with the Lord Mayor to take photos, after which the presents were taken back to be given out again to someone else the following year. Remembering a watch he really wanted to keep, this was another blow to him about the unfairness of the world. Other people have told me this was not true, however, this was his firm memory as he told it to me.

Gwen (Left) with a friend.

Gwen (my mother) was in the girls' home on the corner of Hill Street, placed there at the age of seven as her mother had died. My grandmother had been one of the canary girls working in the munitions factory at Ordnance Rd, Coventry, where the chemicals in the munitions turned her skin yellow. She died in Gulson Road Hospital aged 34 in 1930. She left behind seven children and was having another baby when she died. I am told my grandfather remained sad for the rest of his life.

Gwen's father was unable to cope with the whole family and regretfully placed her and her three brothers in the care of the Council. The three boys went to the infants home, also in Hill Street, before moving on to Hillcrest at seven. Her father died when she was 12. So great was the impact of the homes on her childhood that she made my father promise, he would never put us in one. She seemed to know she was not going to live out a full life. Dad used to say when he was mad with us, (sometimes it didn't take much):

'I shouldn't have promised your mother, I should have put you in a home.'

I used to think we would have been better off, but from what I know now, that possibly was not the case! I also used to think my mother was not dead, or that I was a gypsy princess that they would be coming back for later.

All the children attended Spon Street School and St John's Church on Sundays, as a lot of them were in the choir. This meant going to church three times a day. The girls' home was on the corner of Hill Street, facing Bond's Hospital. It was bombed during the war.

There were many big families in the homes, some parents had child after

49

child, and handed them over to the orphanage as soon as they could. It was quite hard for the children to understand, baby brothers or sisters would come from nowhere and it was greatly upsetting for them.

They often waited for their Mum and Dad to come on the monthly Sunday visit, but time after time they failed to show up. My grandfather and aunts did visit, but he was so unhappy about losing his wife, and having to give four children up that he did not seem to know what to say, and just looked very upset the whole time he was there. The family remained close to each other despite this, the older sisters who had remained at home to look after the baby still mothered the younger ones for a long time. Other families were not that lucky, parents never came.

In both boys' and girls' homes the children were taught good survival skills like darning socks, basic sewing, scrubbing and cleaning, as well as laying a fire, and as they grew up, peeling vegetables, and making sandwiches for the others in the home. These skills stayed with them for life.

It was possibly materially a better life than some children had outside of the homes, as everything was provided for them, however, the love and affection that a close family enjoys was missing. The teasing and camaraderie, and some of them never learned this for the rest of their lives. A kiss and a cuddle were not on the menu!

Discipline was maintained by denying privileges or by face slapping, sometimes the pump, the rubber plimsoll shoes worn in those days, or the cane. However, there was not too much physical punishment. The kids also had the opportunity to go on holiday to the seaside, to Dymchurch in Kent, to Hemsby in Norfolk. Some holidays were spent at Potter's Holiday Camp at Hopton-on-Sea, also in Norfolk, where the children were called Potter's Scamps. This was something that would be out of the question in most Coventry pre-war homes.

This all changed in 1939 when Sir Alfred Herbert, a well known benefactor to Coventry bought Town Thorns – a mansion beyond Brinklow, which he intended to use for city kids to go camping, to experience the countryside and fresh air. When the war started in earnest in 1940, he agreed it could be used for the children of Coventry to be evacuated to safety in the Warwickshire countryside. Sir Alfred kindly gave the mansion to Coventry Corporation in September 1940. It was decided that the best idea would be to combine all of the scattered corporation homes into one, so the move was made to Town Thorns. This was a fortunate thing, as the girls' home in Hill Street was bombed during the blitz.

Eileen, who had been in Town Thorns, was from one of several of the bigger families, told me that they tried to look out for each other, brothers and sisters, but as they were still separated by dormitories this was not easy. In addition, some of the staff had obvious favourites. She still feels for her brother Barry, made to wear an apron through dinner one day as punishment, and sit next to her. It made her cry. The washrooms were upstairs, a huge area with lots of sinks.

Eileen and her husband.

'My flannel and towel was number 9, hanging on a hook, my sister's was 46, and you never forget that sort of thing. They tried to get us out into service or something similar when we were 14. I recall the headmaster taking me to buy a coat for my first live-in job. I was so excited. We went into Coventry and to a Gentlemen's outfitters where he chose for me a serviceable man's coat buttoning down the boys' side - excitement became disappointment and I hated the coat. That was it - we didn't go without but there was no place for finer feelings.' Eileen sang to me the Town Thorns song.

I'm tired of Town Thorns, I want to go home,
It's weeks and weeks and years and years, since I've seen home.
Mummy, Daddy, fetch me home, from this convalescent home,
I've been here for seven years or more, now I want to stay with you.
Goodbye to all the staff, goodbye to all the children,
Goodbye to Mr Smith, and a jolly good shut to you all!

Another Hillcrest old boy told me that when war broke out they went to Town Thorns, and there was a little more mixing of the sexes than there was in Coventry. Though you still did not set foot in the girls' dormitory! He was set to work on some of the jobs needed round the mansion, then sent to work on a nearby farm, missing his last year at school. Gwen, my mother, went into service for the Matron, Miss Floyd.

The extensive grounds at Town Thorns were beautiful, and in the spring, there were thousands of daffodils, enough to make Wordsworth blink. The children were forbidden to play on some parts of the gardens due to this, and they also lent a hand in picking the daffs and making them into bunches to sell outside the Council House to make money for the Corporation to plough back into the costs of running such a large establishment. Moving the children on at working age must have been a bit of a headache, and it seems most of them went into service, or farm work, or sometimes the Army, or other similar institutions. With nowhere to live and no family support, the choices had to be live-in.

At the end of the war, the children still at Town Thorns were moved to Spencer Road, The Grange at Keresley, or Stoke Hill. Again, whilst well cared for, they missed the closeness of home, and sometimes felt in the way.

Coventry Education Committee also had places at Wyre Forest, in Cleobury Mortimer in Shropshire, and Corley Open Air School. A man who had been to Wyre Farm after Town Thorns, told me he was very much happier there. He recalled being severely shepherded in a crocodile to Brinklow church every Sunday, in silence, from Town Thorns. This compared unfavourably to the relaxed strolls across the fields to the church at Wyre Farm, where the staff and pupils chatted and identified birds as well as admiring the view. The unwitting learning was invaluable, and more natural.

Those who had the shared background of Hillcrest, Hill Street, Town Thorns, or Wyre Farm, are getting older, and have mostly recovered from their experiences. Town Thorns, a BEN (Motor Benevolent Charity) unit for those with physical disabilities who have worked for the car industries now occupy the considerable mansion, with its lovely views and peaceful setting. An opportunity to return was given to the old inmates some years ago, and they were able to reminisce together, laughing at shared times, and catching up with the future. Some had even seen the ghost of the legendary grey lady.

There are some, though who were indelibly marked by their time spent in 'care' who will never forgive, or forget. I would like to think we have moved on since then, let us hope so. No doubt, the Council did their best - but nothing replaces a parent - ever. Losing one is something that stays with you for life. Believe me - I know.

Gill Yardley

Acknowledgements

Thank you to Eileen Nicholls for sharing her memories

Bibliography

The Story of a Country Mansion by Dierdre Rishworth

Barbara Davies

Following the success of the dilutee system in the First World War the practice was revived in the Second World War as the men increasingly left the factories to join the armed forces. Barbara was one of those who answered the call for women to work in factories. She and her friend Doreen, living with their respective parents in Sowerby Bridge, Yorkshire, desperately wanted to train as nurses. Both were members of the St. John's Ambulance Brigade and wanted to do their bit to help the war effort. At the end of 1941, when Barbara was seventeen, they applied together to train as nurses at Middlesex Hospital in London. They discovered that they would have to complete a three-month trial period to see if they were suitable for the job and the job was suitable for them, and if they did not pass they were out. During this period there would be no pay and no accommodation provided. Barbara's mother, a widow with two younger daughters to support, took a very pragmatic view of the problem and told her she could not afford to go. She would be unable to give her daughter any financial support and she would not even have the small contribution to the household budget that Barbara was making from her wages. So that was the end of that ambition.

At the time Barbara was working at a mill in the town where wages were low and had previously worked in clothing manufacture. She heard from someone in the mill that recruiting for Armstrong Whitworth Aircraft (AWA) was going on in Hebden Bridge and it was possible to earn up to £5 a week. This seemed a fortune to the lowly paid mill girls. Barbara and Doreen decided to go and apply. They thought that if they worked for a year and saved up, they would be able to support themselves for the three-month period at Middlesex Hospital after all. Full of hope they filled out the forms and as they were both only seventeen they needed the consent of a parent. Barbara's mother signed, but with the caution that she hoped her daughter knew what she was doing. However, Doreen's mother would not sign, as she did not want another child leaving home after the departure of her son for the forces not long before.

Barbara was very disappointed when she heard the news, but decided to go ahead. She was an ambitious young person who could see the limits of living in a small community and needed to widen her horizons. It was the end of 1941 when she sent in her application form and in January 1942 she was on her way to Coventry by train. Although there were other girls travelling on the same errand, she knew no one. When the train reached Coventry she saw a scene of devastation. There was no station, for it had been destroyed in the November blitz of 1940. A van was there to meet the girls and a long and tedious journey was made around the city dropping off girls in ones and twos at houses where they were to lodge. Barbara was amazed at the damage she saw, for Sowerby Bridge had seen nothing of the bombing going on in industrial centres around the country. Eventually she and another girl, Flo, were the last to be deposited at a house in Macdonald Road, Wyken. The people were kind and the house was clean. She and Flo shared a twin-bedded room and got on well together, despite the fact that they had nothing in common. Flo was a good time girl about ten years older than Barbara, wore heavy make-up and went dancing every night. Barbara was an innocent and once the evening meal was over spent her time writing letters and reading in their room. She wrote to everyone she knew, friends and family and earned the nickname of Miss Basildon Bond.

On the first day at the factory they were up early and went out to get the bus. It was pitch black and difficult to find their way in the blackout. They reached the bus stop to find a crowd waiting, rather than a queue. When the bus arrived it was more like a scrum, with elbows flying, to get a place. Flo hustled Barbara aboard and off they went. When they arrived at the factory, a huge place right next to Baginton airport (down what is now Siskin Drive). They were ushered into a room to see the Welfare Officer, Mrs Wilkie Smith. She looked very prim and proper, dressed in twin-set and pearls and her hair looking immaculate. She talked to the girls in a posh middle-class accent, which jarred with Barbara. She told them that they would be issued with overalls and assigned to a gang. She did not explain what they would be doing. Perhaps in her ivory tower, she did not actually know.

They were led into the factory, which was vast and filled with large machines. Production of the Whitley bomber had just finished and they were starting to produce the Lancaster bomber. AWA was a huge factory, made up of three very large sheds joined together, plus offices. Part of the aircraft was assembled in the shed furthest from the airfield and gradually moved through the three sheds, being assembled as it progressed, until the completed aircraft was wheeled out on to the apron at the end, ready to be flown away to RAF air bases.

As the group of girls were taken into the factory on that first day they saw a hive of activity, as men moved about or worked on machines dressed in their sandy-coloured cow gowns. The men made it very plain to the women that they were not welcome. A man came up to them and looked them over to assess them. They were eventually assigned to do a job, but on an ad hoc basis. Barbara was asked if she was doing anything, to which she replied in the negative and a man gave her a box of screws and told her he wanted them made shorter. She had to saw them to the correct size, fix them in a vice and put a die in the machine to grind a new screw. By the time she had done that for an hour, as she said, she was ready to climb up the wall. The work was too repetitive, she preferred some variety to keep her interested.

When it was time for a tea break, labourers came along with long sticks to pick up the men's mashing cans (billycans) that were placed on each machine. They were taken to a point where boiling water came out of pipes and filled up the cans and returned them to the owner's machine. The operator then made his own tea with the water. No one offered the girls a drink, not even water. There was a canteen but the girls could not generally afford to use it, they brought a packed lunch. The toilet facilities were just as inadequate. The women's toilets were adapted for their use, but were very smelly. There was no cloakroom to hang up their coats, so they had to be left in a pile on the benches. It was almost as though the company ignored the prospect of women on the factory floor until they actually arrived.

As AWA was a closed shop, the women had to join the union, in this case the Amalgamated Engineering Union (AEU). When they joined they were told that it was just for the duration of the war, but once over, they were out. Barbara had belonged to a union in the mill, but this was a really large and important union, with a lot of power. Nothing had really changed from the experience of the First World War. The unions did not want women doing what they considered men's jobs and did nothing to make life easier for them.

In those first few weeks the men tried to belittle the women as much as possible, by making a fool of them. They played tricks on them by sending them to the stores for non-existent items, like a rubber hammer or a replacement bulb for a spirit level. It was almost an initiation process that they went through to humiliate them. In fact young apprentices had the same sort of humiliating treatment to go through before they were accepted. They usually fell for these jokes as they did not know any better, but eventually it stopped. Barbara earned another nickname at this time, Little Yorkie.

The promised £5 wages did not materialise, at least not to begin with. When she was doing repetitive jobs making small parts, there was no chance of a high wage. When they were recruiting people to work on a gang making wings for Lancasters, she applied and became a gofer. The gang system was a very effective form of piecework. It consisted of about thirty people making a particular part of the aircraft. The gang was paid a set figure for completing a piece, in Barbara's case a wing. The rate of pay for each member of the gang, was set according to their status. Male engineers received the most and the women received the lowest rates at just over half the men's rate. As Barbara remarked, some of the engineers were very clever at reading the drawings. She admired them for their skill and because there were engineers in her own family. She was sent all over the factory to get this and that and when she was not required for a few minutes she would watch what the men were doing.

The wings were constructed from preformed pieces of metal that fitted together. There were two large panels making the upper and lower casing of the wings and everything was fitted to this. The front edge was called the leading edge and the rear was called the trailing edge. Bracing ribs were fixed between the two panels to strengthen the structure and petrol tanks were contained within the wings. There were two engines in each wing and the metal casing was shaped to accommodate them. All parts were bolted or riveted together. Ladders were used to gain access to the wings as they were being worked upon. There was no bother about Health and Safety; people just took care of their own safety. Sheets of aluminium were riveted on, but at the leading and trailing edge of each sheet they were always screwed and peened to give extra strength and to stop vibration. At each stage an inspector would examine every rivet, bolt and joint. If he was not satisfied it had to be done again.

On one occasion Barbara was assigned the job of remaking a hole for a new rivet, after it was rejected by an inspector. By this time she had changed her job within the gang to a sagger's mate. If the hole was too large you could not just put a larger rivet in its place, as it would not fit in with the depth of the others. A new piece of metal had to be used as a patch and another hole drilled for the rivet. Barbara went off to get a new piece of metal from the tinsmiths. The tinsmiths union was the only one in the factory that never accepted women members. The coppersmiths were initially opposed to women in their union too, but eventually relented when they found how quick and nimble the girls were at bending the copper piping used as conduits to carry wires within the bombers. The tinsmiths, however, were adamant and obstructive. When Barbara went to get her piece of metal the men were on their tea break. She said she wanted a small square of metal for a repair and they replied that she would have to wait. Not noted for her patience, she said that she would do it herself. They warned her not to touch it, but she went over to a big bin of metal bits, selected a piece and inserted it into a guillotine and pulled the lever. The machine made a loud 'clunk' as it cut one side, 'clunk' on the next and so on until she had all four sides cut. This roused the men to action and she had to run to get away. They were not concerned about loss of production due to their obduracy, only their own privileges. She told the gang what had happened and they hoped it would be forgotten. However, she was called in to see the superintendent who reprimanded her and she was forbidden to do such a thing again. It caused a furore, but of course strikes were not allowed, as it was considered a treasonable offence in wartime.

Around twelve to thirteen bombers were completed every week. They were wheeled out on to the apron and women pilots came to deliver them to the RAF. These girls were very glamorous, like film stars. They usually dressed the part too. Barbara admired them very much, although some could be quite imperious. They were generally girls from wealthy families who had learned to fly before the war. They would taxi the bombers on to the runway and fly off to some distant airfield.

As production speeded up at the factory more girls were taken on later in 1942. These girls were hosiery workers from Hinckley and already used to working with their hands doing very fine work. They soon became expert at riveting and could work far more quickly in confined spaces than the men.

It was soon realised that these girls could be a great asset to the workforce. Their skill could increase the work rate and that meant more money for the rest of the gang too. When the Hinckley girls saw the conditions that the first intake of women had to work under, they were not impressed. Very soon they had a cloakroom and new toilets through the representation of their union. These girls were members of the Transport and General Workers Union (TGWU), a large union and rival to the AEU. The AEU, being the main union in the factory before the women arrived, considered that the TGWU were poaching their female members. Jack Jones, the TGWU General Secretary in Coventry used persuasion to get its members improved conditions. Women realised the power they wielded in the factory with increased numbers.

Periodically, Mrs Wilkie Smith, the Welfare Officer at the factory, called the girls in to check on how they were getting on. As Barbara waited to see her on one occasion, another girl was being interviewed who looked in a dreadful state with boils all over her face, looking pale and exhausted. She was in tears, complaining about the terrible digs she lived in, with a damp bed and the only food provided was cold and had to be eaten straight from the tin. The house was in Radford and she wanted to be moved. Instead of sympathising with the poor girl, Mrs Wilkie Smith, looking perfectly groomed as usual, said to the girl, 'Don't you know there is a war on?'

Barbara was incensed and intervened on the girl's behalf, saying that she should not have to put up with such conditions, war or not. The girl, Jane, was sent to the doctor who found her severely malnourished. She was sent home for three weeks to recover, but had to return. Barbara sought her out when she returned and found she came from Hebden Bridge, not far from Barbara's home. They decided to find digs together at a house Jane had heard of in Broad Lane owned by a woman and her adult son, whom she doted on.

Barbara 1st left, Jane 3rd left outside Finham Hostel.

59

They were certainly happier there, although their room only held a Morrison shelter, which was used as a table during the day and under which they slept at night, plus a couple of chairs. They only stayed a couple of months, when following an interview they moved into a hostel in Finham. The hostel covered a large site around Brentwood Avenue. Long huts were used for accommodation and they had all the benefits of the leisure facilities. There was a dining hall, sports hall, dance hall, billiards room, small library and a sick bay. Their sleeping area was very limited and Barbara cannot believe how much space prisoners get today in comparison. She and Jane were like sisters living in the hostel and cycling to the factory each day where Jane also worked on wings, though not in Barbara's gang.

Jane (right) working on wings.

As they began working on the wings, climbing up ladders they needed trousers for ease of access. They had to buy their own bib and brace overalls, as the wrap around type they were originally issued with was not suitable. Barbara's wages fluctuated according to the amount of work that could be done. If they had a really good week, rather than having a larger sum, the foreman would hold some back, called, 'putting it in the back of the book.' This was used to boost up a poor week and evened out the final sum they received each week. If the rate fixer thought you were making too much money, he could lower the rate, which seems a disincentive to work hard. Here are a few examples of the sort of wages the girls were earning in the last few months of the war. Week ending 6th April 1945 the gross wage was £8 15s 5d minus tax of £2 7s; 24th August 1945 the gross wage was £7 10s 2d minus tax of £1 14s. Some weeks the wage was far less than this and the tax was a sizeable proportion of the gross pay.

When Barbara had been working at AWA for a while, they began to use frozen rivets in the wings that she worked on. They could be used for half an hour before they had to be put back in the freezer and another batch taken out. It made it easier to put the rivets in the holes and as they warmed, the metal expanded and made a tighter fit. Barbara has kept the tin box (made by the tinsmiths) with a double lift-up lid with two compartments for rivets. Someone had etched MISS PRIM on one lid and BABS BUMPS EM HOME on the other. It illustrates the skill of the tinsmiths and the type of rivets that were used; one eighth of an inch was the usual size.

In the early days in Coventry Barbara was rather lonely and decided to contact the St. John's Ambulance Brigade to see if she could help. She became part of the safety team at the factory, although it was not always popular with her colleagues, as occasionally she would have to go for practice and it would hold up the production of the gang. They practiced for a gas attack, where she had to wear oilskins and hose people down. As she is barely five feet tall, the all-encompassing clothing quite overwhelmed her. As she says now, 'You would not have stood a dog's chance in hell if it had happened.' They had a primitive decontamination unit, which would have been totally inadequate in the event of an attack. She joined the ambulance service of the Hospital Saturday Fund to continue using the medical skills she had learned in Yorkshire. She helped out at weekends, when they attended accidents, falls, hangings and much more. As she says, they were the paramedics of the day. The city owned two ambulances that were manned by members of the Fire Brigade. The Hospital Saturday Fund owned a fleet of ambulances, some of which were used as patient transport on a daily basis and some were fully equipped for emergency use. They were manned by St. John's Ambulance personnel on a voluntary basis.

The war in Europe ended in May 1945, but production of aircraft continued until soon after V J Day in August. One day the women were told that they would all be sacked on the following Thursday. This only applied to the women, of course, not the men. Barbara went to the union representative and asked him, 'What happens now?' His reply was, 'Go back where you came from.' They could not have cared less what happened to these women who had worked so hard over several years. There was not even a thank you, nor did they pay the fare for them to get home if that was the intention. The women had a feeling of total rejection. If they had been in the forces, their fares would have been paid and they would have had more holidays, instead of one week annual leave and one day at Christmas, Easter and Whitsun. They were not even allowed to go home for the weekend in case they could not return on time.

When Barbara had signed up as a dilutee at the end of 1941 she thought it was just for a year and she would be free to pursue a nursing career. However, she discovered that she could not leave when she wanted and had to stick it out for the duration of the war. When the end came she was not sure what she wanted. She knew she wanted more than Sowerby Bridge could offer, making clothes or back in the mill. She went home to think about her next move.

Jane was good at sewing and wanted to stay in Coventry, where she soon found a job using her skill. Barbara returned to Coventry and found a job at the Coventry Radiator and Presswork (Cov Rad). On her first day she was taken to a press machine and shown what was required. By the side of the machine was a large bin containing round metal blanks called bendix plates. They had to be put in the press and a lever pulled down with a loud 'clonk.' When the lever was lifted up again, the metal had been shaped. She stuck it until the midday break and like her first day at AWA she became bored with the repetitive nature of the job. She also found that she had difficulty reaching the plates in the bin once she was half way down, because of her short stature.

Finding the foreman she told him she wanted to leave. He told her she could not leave, just the same as her wartime service. Never afraid to stand up to authority, she told him that she would wreck his machine if not allowed to leave. He called her bluff, so she marched back to the press, put in two plates and pulled the lever. It made a loud CLANG. He screamed at her, 'Get your coat.' She was free.

Barbara stayed in Coventry where she married and had children. Her drive and ambition led her to train as a teacher of needlework and domestic science. Two of the places she worked were Coventry Technical College and Coundon Court School. She has lived in Coventry for nearly seventy years, but her heart still hankers for Yorkshire and Sowerby Bridge.

Lynn Hockton

62

Interviewed January 2011

Thank you to Barbara for sharing her vivid memories of working as a dilutee.

Irene Ward

Irene Ward was born a month before the armistice was signed by Germany which brought about the end of the First World War. She was born at the family home in Matlock Road, Foleshill and was one of 12 children. After a few years the family decided to move to Newfield Road where Irene attended Narrow Lane School. The family moved again some years later to Lowther Street, where Irene attended Frederick Bird School.

It was from here that Irene joined the Girl Guides in Chapel Street in the city centre. Irene's future husband, Thomas Terry, lived with his family in Chapel Street. She was 15 years old and Tom was 16 and they would meet each other regularly as she left Girl Guides in the evening. A few years after finishing school, Tom was working as a delivery driver and Irene was working at Cash's ribbon weaving factory. For the next five years they courted until at last, in 1939, Irene agreed to marry Tom.

The wedding took place on the 26th August 1939 and they had a house ready to move into, which was situated in Elgar Road. The wedding was only a week before war was declared and on the following day the city's sirens were tested. However, as Irene and Tom had been so distracted they did not realise that it was only a test, and so spent the evening hiding underneath the stairs, very frightened.

After the beginning of the Second World War, life was to change dramatically. Rationing was introduced at the beginning of 1940 and by the autumn night-time bombings by German planes became a regular occurrence. The sound of the sirens filled people with absolute fear as there was no indication of the extent of the bombing or how many casualties would be caused. Irene remembers distinctly that the incendiary bombs sounded like bells gently ringing as they fell; a beautiful sound considering the devastating result.

On the night of the 14th November 1940 bombing, the moon was full and bright. People said to one another 'oh look they've got a good run tonight,' not realising how right they were. That night Irene and Tom had been to the pictures to watch a film and had returned home for dinner. Irene was cooking pilchards for dinner and just as she set it on the table the sirens sounded. They abandoned their dinner and quickly ran to the shelter next door. The planes started to fly overhead and the distinctive 'bell' sound could be heard as incendiary bombs fell to the ground. In the shelter they tried to make conversation over the noise, but it was difficult as most of the time was spent listening to whether the bombs were dropping nearby. Irene described it as 'a nightmare, an utter fear' and this particular night the fear was at its peak. Within hours a bomb had landed in the Sewell Highway area, near Tom and Irene's house. The noise of the bomb exploding was immense, causing them to climb out of the shelter to see where it had landed. The impact of the bomb had blown the lock off the front door of the house and it was swinging open. After this experience Irene became very concerned about the safety of her mother and insisted on making the journey to her mother's house in Radford to check that she was all right. They made the journey through the constant bombing and stopped on the way in public shelters for safety when necessary. The air was filled with smoke and there were fires all around, but they kept on walking and finally arrived at the house in Radford. They found the windows had been smashed due to the impact of nearby bombs. There was the strange sight of little birds flying in and out of the house and sitting on the furniture. The family were all unhurt but still shaken by the night's events. Finally in the early hours of the morning the all-clear sounded.

The next morning Tom and Irene made their way back home. There was the eerie sight of people wandering around, exhausted. The water mains had been hit during the night, so many people were looking for water, either to drink or to put out fires. There were still fires blazing and rubble-covered parts of the street, it looked like the end of the world. The air was thick with smoke and the people looked weary and broken as they walked through the damaged streets. Tom went to look at some that had happened near their home, but was quickly moved away by the wardens, as there were unexploded bombs.

This was not the only bombing raid that occurred in Coventry, the sirens sounded regularly and there were too many nights when Irene huddled in the shelter. Tom worked the night shift on most nights in an engineering job or guarding the factory as a member of the Home Guard. This meant that many nights Irene stayed in the shelter with her neighbours worrying about Tom's safety. On one particular night after the sirens had sounded,

Irene heard Tom returning home. He was running up the garden path and suddenly he threw his bike up against the shelter and jumped inside just as a bomb landed very close to the house, shaking the earth violently. After this series of bombings in Coventry, Irene and her family were growing more and more concerned about her mother's safety and so the decision was made to evacuate their mother to the countryside, in Leicestershire.

In 1942 Irene found out that she was pregnant. It was a difficult time to be pregnant, with air raids and rationing, but she bravely carried on and was able to give birth to a healthy baby boy that they named Bob. In order to give birth safely and without the threat of danger, Irene was evacuated for six days to a hospital in Bidford-on-Avon and afterwards was able to return home to Coventry with her little baby, Bob. In order to keep Bob and Tom healthy, Irene used most of her rations on them and soon began to lose a great deal of weight. Her usual weight was 8 stone, but she found that she had dropped down to 5 stone and she was unable to find any clothes to fit her.

In 1945 Irene became pregnant again. The amount of air raids had declined steadily and by April 1945, the announcement finally came that everyone had been waiting for, the end of the war. Everyone was happy; street parties were held all over the city and many people were dressed up in fancy dress. Tables were set out in the street and neighbours made jellies, cakes and sandwiches. Parties were held for many weeks afterwards.

However, after the war life still remained difficult. To her surprise Irene gave birth to twins, Maureen and David, as she had not known it would be twins. As there was still rationing this would make it difficult for Irene who expected to be looking after only one baby. To make matters worse Tom was called up for the Air Force and had to leave for Blackpool for 10 days and he was not there for the birth of the twins. He came back on compassionate leave to see the babies, but was then requested to leave for Ceylon for 12 months. During this time Irene had to raise the three children alone. It was the most difficult time she had experienced so far, and to this day she has no idea how she managed.

Tom finally returned in 1946 on the day of the twins' first birthday. Irene went to the station twice to see if he had arrived, but Tom was very late. She returned home and waited up, trying to keep the babies awake to see him, but they all fell asleep. At 2am she heard Tom walking up the path to the front door, he was finally home. She remembers he walked into the house, put down his bag and fell asleep in the chair in the living room without even taking his coat off.

Charlotte Harper

Thank you to Irene for sharing her memories

Pat Coleman

Pat Coleman's parents made the move to Coventry from the Rhondda Valley in 1939 when Pat was eleven years old. Due to the war, Pat was evacuated to South Wales almost as soon as she arrived, to stay with relatives and complete her education. Back in Coventry at the end of 1942 she began a course at Underwood's Secretarial College in Warwick Row, which lasted a year. Miss Samways was the Principal of the college and it was she who taught typing. Pat was taught to touch type, where the keys were blank, but the layout of the keyboard was on the wall at eye level. They typed to the music of Norwegian mazurkas, which set up a rhythm. Miss Samways carried a cane as she progressed through the room, checking the girls as they typed. She would whack the knuckles of any girl who went wrong. Pat's course was paid for by her father and she left with an RSA typing certificate, with a speed of 65 words a minute and a Pitman's shorthand certificate at 120 words a minute. She was recommended for the post of junior shorthand typist at the end of 1943 when Sidney Snape, the solicitor, asked Miss Samways advice.

The solicitors' office was situated in Little Park Street at the time, as their original premises in the Quadrant had been requisitioned by the military during the war. The Little Park Street premises left a lot to be desired, as it was in a poor state of repair, with few conveniences when it came to running an efficient office. There were no facilities for making drinks and Pat as the most junior member of staff was required to go across the road to the Freemason's Lodge twice a day, to fetch a tray of coffee in the morning and tea in the afternoon, prepared by the caretaker, Mrs Robinson. Functions were frequently held at the Lodge and as fruit was in short supply, Mrs Robinson would give Pat a bag of leftover fruit after such occasions.

The staff consisted of Sidney Snape, the senior partner; Gilbert Richards, the junior partner; Horace Farren, who worked on conveyances; Henry Merryman, the senior clerk whose job entailed finishing off work started by the senior members of staff, and three female shorthand typists of which Pat was the most junior. As far as the pecking order was concerned she was at the bottom and subject to taking orders from all the others. Twice a week she was sent by the other two shorthand typists, to the bakers shop in Little

Park Street. On Wednesdays and Fridays they made lovely fruitcakes and Pat had to queue to buy one, not for herself, but for the other two women at the office. She would like to have bought one for her mother, who would willingly have paid the 3s 6d (17.5p), but patrons could only have one cake at a time.

Pat and the other shorthand typists were required to carry their typewriters and put them in the walk-in safe in Mr Snape's room on the ground floor each night and retrieve them each morning when they came in. This was not so bad for the women on the ground floor, but Pat's office was upstairs and the old-fashioned typewriters were very heavy. After a while of doing this Pat asked Gilbert Richards why it was necessary to go through this operation every night when there was virtually no bombing any longer. His reply was that it was a form of time-keeping check, as Mr Snape would know what time they started and when they left. During the Assizes Pat often worked until 9pm with no overtime paid, but that was a different matter.

Pat generally worked for Gilbert Richards, sometimes accompanying him to the Magistrates Court. The offices were heated by open fires during the winter months, so when Mr Richards went to court he would ask Pat to keep his fire going for his return. On one occasion she was asked to do this as usual, but as she bent over to tend the fire the marble mantelpiece, which was piled up with weighty law books, fell on her head. She called out and Henry Merryman came rushing in. Instead of relieving her of mantel and books, he declared that he knew that this was going to happen. He told her to stay where she was and rushed downstairs to fetch Sidney Snape to see what had happened. Mr Snape, who had lost a leg in the First World War, came stomping up the stairs. When he saw what had occurred he said, 'Give her an Aspirin and a cup of tea and let her sit down for an hour. She will be all right.' No thank you for saving the precious books and no help to get her out of her predicament, it was Henry Merryman who lifted the books off and removed the mantelpiece.

One of the duties of the junior was to deliver the post to the other local solicitors, which could mean an extensive walk all around the city centre in all types of weather. Pat soon learned of the practice of the local juniors who would meet up each day in the Geisha Café in Hertford Street at a given time, to share their news and exchange correspondence over a welcome cup of tea. This was a far more sensible plan than girls rushing around all over the place covering the same ground. Their bosses had no idea what was going on, but it served the same purpose and the documents reached their destination safely.

Pat had been working at the solicitors for some time and as her wages were not generous she would have liked a pay rise. She was mad about the singer Frank Sinatra and used as much of her wages as she could afford buying his records. She even walked or cycled from her home in Canley to save her wages for this purpose. Although wages were low, when members of staff were due to have their annual holiday they were called into Mr Snape's office where he would wish them a very good holiday. Not only did they get a week's holiday pay, but also the train or coach fare to the holiday destination.

Pat worked at the solicitors for five years, a period in her life she would not have missed, where she learned a lot about life in general. Apart from improving her shorthand and typing skills she also learned to sew legal documents. She admired Mr Richards for his dedication to his clients. Pat remarked that solicitors hold people's future in their hands and that the advice given often saved going to litigation. Sidney Snape was very knowledgeable about the law. When a case for Gilbert Richards came up during Pat's time there, Mr Snape remembered a similar case many years before. He directed Pat to return to the basement of their offices in The Quadrant, where documents were stored and told her to look for a date in 1928. He remembered having to go into the office to work on this case on Easter Monday 1928. She found the papers he required and brought them back to Little Park Street, where they were of great assistance to Gilbert Richards in preparing the current case. Sidney Snape travelled from his home in Stratford-upon-Avon every day, even during the war. Gilbert Richards often consulted him and took his advice on a case.

Pat always had a wish to become a nurse, but her father discouraged her, as he wanted her to remain at home. However, Pat applied to a training hospital in Exeter in the hope of getting a place. She waited anxiously for a reply over the following week, but nothing arrived. Eventually her next-door neighbour asked if she was waiting for a letter, to which Pat replied in the affirmative. She informed Pat that the letter had come a couple of weeks before and that her father had destroyed it. Pat confronted her father and he admitted what he had done. He told her that he thought she was being selfish to think of leaving her mother, as she was all she had. Pat knew, however, that it was her father who could not bear to let her go.

When Pat's family had moved to Coventry from Wales, their first home was in Wyken Croft. They had never had a bathroom before so it was quite a novelty. Pat remembers the geyser in the bathroom frightening her to death. Her mother always wanted a new three-piece-suite and as furniture was in short supply she settled for one in green. Pat, an only child, had been evacuated to Wales and her parents were on their own during the worst of the air raids. Her father was an ARP warden and out on duty when an air raid began, so Pat's mother went down into the shelter on her own for the night. The bombing was very severe and when she came out in the morning, their house and those on either side were completely destroyed. Pat's mother, who was very superstitious, swore that if it had not been for that green suite, they would never have been bombed. Since then no member of the family has ever had green furnishings.

Following the destruction of their home in Wyken Croft, they were allocated a house in Edyth Road, not far away. The family had some very good friends who lived in Forknell Avenue, Wyken, whom Pat called Auntie Janet and Uncle Bill. One day, when Pat was home, she and her mother went to visit these friends. Uncle Bill had banked up the fire before going out, but when Pat's mother saw the fire she thought it needed stirring up to create some flames, which she liked. She picked up the poker and was just about to attack it, when quick-thinking Auntie Janet, who knew her husband would not be pleased with anyone touching it, said she had heard somewhere that it was bad luck to poke the fire in someone else's house. That stopped Pat's mother immediately and she bustled off into the kitchen to put the kettle on. Pat asked Auntie Janet if it was true what she had just said about the fire, she replied, 'No, but don't tell your mother.'

Pat has a great sense of humour and an excellent memory for funny things that happened in the past. She has been married and widowed twice and has a daughter, Julia, who became a nurse and midwife. Julia always wanted to be a nurse, but like her mother was wrongly advised about her career, this time by the school careers' officer. She trained in catering initially at

71

Henley College and spent six months in Germany, but after she married and had two sons, she was determined to train as a nurse. She spent 22 years on the district as a midwife, and was later asked to train others to become midwives at Coventry University. Her change of career was made possible by the altered attitude to training and further education, which was not available in Pat's younger years.

Lynn Hockton

Thank you to Pat for sharing her memories.
Interview conducted June 2010.

Brenda Stone – Missionary Nurse

Brenda was born at home in Walsgrave Road, Coventry, in 1926. One of her earliest recollections is of watching the airship R101 fly over. In 1930, the family, including Brenda, her mother and father and her baby sister, moved to a new house in Mellowdew Road, where another sister was born in 1933.

Brenda's first taste of school was a hut off Wyke Road, then at the age of six years she moved to Stoke Council School in Briton Road, which she considers to have been a good school.

In 1937 the family moved to Stretton-on-Dunsmore, to fulfil her father's desire to have a smallholding. The girls were delighted by the move, however, their mother was not so happy as conditions were primitive compared to Mellowdew Road. She insisted that mains electricity had to be connected; this was arranged and their house became the first in Stretton to have mains electricity. Water had to be collected daily from an outdoor tap, which was connected to a well. Their father kept chickens, geese and pigs; the girls had dogs, cats and rabbits – an idyllic childhood indeed.

At the age of eleven, Brenda passed a scholarship for Rugby High School. She was the only girl in Stretton to attend this school. There were three boys attending the grammar school, so they all travelled together, but of course in those days the two schools were totally separate.

During the Second World War relatives of the Stone family came out to Stretton to sleep and thus avoid the bombing in Coventry.

At the age of sixteen Brenda left school and started work in Coventry Income Tax office, where she remained for about two years. She then joined the Auxiliary Territorial Service (ATS) around 1944/5 and was sent to Pontefract Barracks for training. Brenda had been baptised as a baby in Stoke St. Michael's church and had attended Sunday School, but had not become greatly involved in the church. However, at Pontefract she formed a friendship with a girl whose father was a vicar and became sufficiently interested to be confirmed in the parish church. After completing the training course, Brenda was posted to Rugby and billeted in one of the Rugby School houses. She was given clerical work to do, which was rather boring, however, life soon became more exciting when she was posted to Egypt, probably in 1946. Although the work was still clerical, she had time to visit museums, cinemas, and other places and as there were far more soldiers than ATS girls, escorts were always available. Another pastime was playing hockey on a pitch of firm sand. Brenda attended the Anglican Cathedral in Cairo and had the opportunity to visit a Church Missionary Society hospital in a downtown area. Brenda left the ATS in 1947 and returned to Stretton.

Whilst in Egypt Brenda decided that she definitely wanted to do Christian missionary work and that the best way forward was to become a nurse. She commenced training in 1948 at the Queen Elizabeth Hospital in Birmingham. The work was hard and the sisters in charge were very strict. Training to become a nurse took three years; during a fourth year Brenda worked as a staff nurse in the operating theatres. Her normal shift was 4.30pm to midnight (later if necessary), plus emergencies. Her next training was in midwifery at the British Hospital in Woolwich, London. After this, Brenda moved to the opposite side of the River Thames to Poplar, where she worked for six months as a student midwife, working with the nursing sisters of St. John the Divine. Most births took place at home and the midwives travelled around by bicycle. It was now 1953, Coronation year and the people of Poplar threw themselves into the occasion; some even painted the whole exterior of their houses red, white and blue!

Brenda now returned to Coventry to spend a few weeks in Casualty at Coventry & Warwickshire Hospital, stitching wounds, etc.; then a short time at Moorfields Eye Hospital to gain further experience.

She went on to her missionary training by the Society for the Propagation of the Gospel. Brenda was one of six students from the University Mission to Central Africa. They were based at the College of the Ascension in Selly Oak, Birmingham for two terms, to learn the Swahili language, do some bible studies, learn how to keep fit, cope with hygiene and more.

With her training completed Brenda set off in September 1954, on a Union Castle liner, for a one month's voyage via the Mediterranean and the Suez Canal to Dar-es-Salaam, Tanganyika (now Tanzania). Here she transferred to a small ship down the African coast to Lindi. This was followed by a 100 mile journey by lorry to the Masasi diocese. Brenda was posted to the Lulindi mission station as one of five missionaries – one doctor, three nurses and one priest; the domestic staff consisted of local people. There was a 100-bed hospital, catering for men, women and children. Mothers often stayed with their children to help with their care. Conditions were somewhat primitive, however, having lived in Stretton, Brenda did not find this too much of a shock! The hospital had a thatched roof, only the operating theatre had glass windows, the wards merely had shutters and instruments were sterilized over a fire. There was a school of nursing, one of the first in the country, where local girls could train from the age of sixteen years. They were taught in English, despite only having learned a little English at school. The local staff was paid by the diocese; the missionaries were paid from London at £30 per year plus their keep. The money was mainly spent on postage stamps, but sometimes it was given to the poor.

In 1970 Brenda moved into Health Work. The World Health Organisation had become concerned at the number of babies who died after they were weaned. Although they had a low birth weight by western standards, the majority were perfectly healthy whilst they were breast fed. The obvious conclusion was that the food was not sufficiently nutritious. Someone had to get out into the villages and show the people what could be done, but the problem was how to get there?

Brenda (right) with two local nurses.

The mission became possible when the Oxfam organisation provided a Land Rover complete with driver. Brenda could now provide a once a month clinic in an area with a fifty-mile radius; these took place wherever possible, in the church, the school, or just an open place under a tree. She took a very big pan and a supply of mugs; the leaves of the local cashew nut trees served as spoons. The staple diet of the local people was a type of porridge made up of maize and water, cooked over an open fire. So Brenda started with this porridge in her big pan, but to it she added anything that would add extra nutrition, including peas, beans, honey, milk, left-over vegetables, ground peanuts, etc. She gave a mug of this improved porridge to each child and they loved it, as it was really good.

The young children were weighed each time there was a clinic, so that their parents could see their progress. Brenda had a supply of trousers which acted as slings to hang each child from the scales. Their weight was recorded on a chart, which their parents took home and brought to the next clinic. Brenda also cut up old envelopes and wrote on them the date of the next clinic; surprisingly, few people ever lost these items despite living in mud houses with thatched roofs. The usual storage place was inside their hymn book.

After twenty years in Africa, fifteen at the hospital and five at the clinics, Brenda decided it was time to return to England; her parents were becoming elderly and needing some assistance. She moved in with her parents who were most welcoming. She was shocked to find how extravagant and wasteful people were. She went to work at Whitley Hospital, at first on the orthopaedic ward and then on the geriatric ward. This was inadequately staffed, particularly on the evening shift when there was only three staff to thirty patients; as Brenda said 'absolute toil.' After four years there, Brenda applied for a post at Windmill Road clinic; when asked if she had a car she replied, 'No, but I've got a bike.' This work was much less stressful, mainly dealing with mothers and children and she remained there until retiring at the age of sixty.

To Brenda retirement was no problem! She is a committed worker at St. Margaret's Church on Ball Hill and is the church's representative on the Christian Aid committee; she also supports campaigns to benefit cyclists and other activities. She still rides her bicycle to some extent and tends her garden on Shakespeare Street Gardens. She says that she is slowing down, but she certainly still keeps really busy.

Kathleen Barker

Thank you to Brenda for sharing her memories

A Child's View of Christmas

Once upon a time, when Greyfriars Green was all one big blousy piece of grass, not dissected by the road to the station, Coventry's Christmas lights were put up there. There were garlanded coloured bulbs all round the hedges at the sides, and running bunnies in a now-you-see-me-now-you-don't fashion. Peacocks whose middles lit up and went out in sequence, and hardboard cut-outs of nursery rhymes lit up to good effect. You could run behind these to see how they worked. Some of the lights had been borrowed from Leamington.

The Coventry lights were not as showy as now, nor switched on by anyone special. However, it was still a treat to go and see them. I thought it was miles from somewhere we called 'downtown', so it's amazing now to realize how close everything is, unless you have a full shopping bag! They did have real live bands playing carols though, which was such a treat. Greyfriars Green also had downstairs toilets underneath Sir Thomas White's statue. I used to wonder how it did not collapse in, and could imagine sitting there and a statue arriving in your lap complete with lawn!

Norway always sent Coventry a large spruce tree that was erected in Broadgate, with a star atop. That was when Lady Godiva was an island unto herself, hallowed and mysterious, and giggly rude. Opposite, outside Holy Trinity would be the crib, with baby Jesus in his nothings, straw strewn around, and the rest of the Nativity scene. Not harmed by anyone, or fenced off or glassed in, it was unheard of then that such things would be vandalized.

We always went to the Pantomime at the Hippodrome, though I was never sure whether it was the Hippodrome at the Pantomime. Both delicious words, as was the experience. Dad worked for the Corporation buses and the Panto was a yearly treat for us kids. We were always 'up in the gods' and Dad grumbled about it, but we loved it - queued up steps by the side door that went on for ever, we had to come out on the roof surely? Like David Balfour in *Kidnapped*. It was like sitting in a giant ashtray, and the steps sloped down so steeply a Sherpa each would have been reassuring. The boys spat on those lucky enough to be in the circle, or if they had good aim, the stalls as well, we'd be content to let our ice-cream tubs slip over the side - oh dear! When the ballet part came on I would take myself off to the toilet, and it fascinated me that it was daylight in there, yet dark in the theatre! The other thing that perturbed me was our doctor's head on the safety curtain, although when we went to see him after Christmas there was not even a join! It was years later I realized it was Shakespeare - but I am telling you he was a dead ringer for Dr White in Rotherham Road. We had circular coloured badges to wear on our coats with our names and who we belonged to, like unclaimed evacuees. If you kept twisting it round, the button came off as well as the badge.

Afterwards we were herded up and taken to the Drill Hall on the site now occupied by IKEA, for a Christmas party. Ladies with hats and hat pins that went in one side of their heads and out the other without a sign of blood, wielded huge hot teapots and made sure we had sandwiches before the cakes. Manners decreed that we never took the first or last cake, discipline was needed to keep to this. We had been told if we were offered any of the sandwiches that were left to bring them home. There were five of us, always hungry. The sandwiches would be fried the next day for our breakfast - nasty if they were fish paste, but better than nothing. The days of health and hygiene were a long way off - it seemed fun in those days.

The entertainment was always Charlie Chaplin, or Buster Keeton, and deadly boring to me. The excitement was in making our own shadow shapes on the walls when the light was off. I could do a good moving camel, and a rabbit if pushed. A smack round the ear was the punishment if I was spotted. Leaving the Drill Hall with a present apiece, we would go home via Greyfriars Green and get another look at the festive lights, and hear the carols, there was an air of excitement after a very full day, and seeing the illuminations again was a great ending to it all.

Christmas at school always began with the school nativity play. I longed to be Mother Mary, but Margaret McConkey got the part. She was tall and blonde, and already had a blue dress. Alan Jones was Joseph, with a tea towel tied round his head, held there by his striped snake belt. Jesus was played by Gloria Mapp's walkie-talkie doll, and Margaret got to hold it. I was greener than Greyfriars! On the day of the dress rehearsal disaster struck. Somehow the doll was dropped, and couldn't be saved even by its swaddling clothes. There was a loud crack, and a big silence, followed by an elongated maaammaa as the talkie bit fell out of the doll's broken back. I was secretly glad. She would get it from Mrs Mapp, a fearsome woman with steel curlers and arms permanently crossed over her chest, who took no prisoners. Her battles on behalf of her large clan were legendary. For the actual performance a rolled up sheet had to suffice for the baby - safe if dropped by a butter-fingered Mary. Alan Jones had his card marked too. Before the Christmas play I used to let him catch me in kiss chase, that wasn't going to happen again, after he put his arms round the Virgin Mary.

Playing the part of the innkeeper I had to say, 'no room at the inn' and Dad joked that it must have been hard learning my lines - which made everyone but me laugh. I had to wear pillow ticking and thump Gramp's walking stick on the ground. Of course on the day I froze to the spot and could not say the five words. My family never forgot though, they had longer memories than the elephant up the pole in Broadgate, where we always met in those days. On another occasion, I had to be a Christmas pudding complete with custard, as I was the fattest in the class I never saw the funny side of it - my sister got to be a snowflake in a white dress with cotton wool sewn on here and there.

On Christmas Day Dad would carve the turkey, and he always asked 'Who had the leg last year? Five kids and two legs, meant some people lied and some forgot, as the legs were coveted. I just realized breast meat was nicer and easier to eat! We also had a bottle of red and brown sauce, just at Christmas. The pudding was special as it was set alight and then yielded money except for Dad who had a button wrapped in paper. I was mystified why this only happened to him, and felt hurt on his behalf, which made him laugh at me, always the sensitive one.

In the afternoon we settled round the Ferguson 9inch television screen to watch High Noon, lining up chestnuts on our hearth to cook. As Gary Cooper moseyed down the wide main street looking for cowboys and a rail to tie his horse to, our own shoot out started as the chestnuts exploded one by one and ricocheted towards the brown, cold Rexine settee, pebbledashing it just below our feet. One year we put them in the oven instead, but they still went bang all over the place.

Another Christmas Annette Mills died - the operator of Muffin the Mule and Prudence Kitten. I was worried that Muffin had strutted his last stuff, rather than concerned at the death of his mistress. Such were the powers of my belief in dear old Muffin playing the fool. Despite being a big family, Christmases were usually good, all the stops being pulled out and an armistice on shouting and smacks for Christmas Day at least. I was a pencil box kind of a child and impatient to boot, and really coveted a Rollex red pencil case. To my delight, it was amongst my presents. Forcing the rolled top over my new striped rubber and crayons, the thing snapped, and rolled forever inside the back. Despite some dodgy fish glue, it was never restored.

One year Dad made us cradles out of oval shaped orange boxes, with a half oval for the hood. We were told to keep out of the shed, but went in anyway, and discovered them mid-construction. A pair of upset parents told us they were for some orphans somewhere, and it served us right for looking. We were amazed then on Christmas morning to find a red rockered crib clad in blue with tiny red rosebuds all over, with a doll waiting inside. It seemed to be fated though, as horseplaying with my brother one day, he fell on to the crib, flattening the balsa wood and blue padded cradle to smithereens. I remember one year Gran bought me a black doll, I loved the Harriet Beecher Stowe story of *Uncle Tom's Cabin*, and she used to say, 'you're like Topsy, you didn't come, you growed!'

As the family grew, and so did we, Gran took to buying us liberty bodices. She felt that by getting clothes she was helping the economy, and she also wanted us to be warm. Well, liberty bodice was a real misnomer. It went after your vest and before your petticoat, and had funny rubber buttons along the bottom. It was fleecy and clumsy looking, and left us feeling constrained. What was worse was that Gran wanted to see our faces when we opened presents, she said for her it was the best part. Trying to get excited about a liberty bodice or two has marked me for life. It went on for years. I find myself saying now, 'I like to open my presents in private, if you don't mind,' just in case it is another liberty bodice moment.

At around twelve years old, I had a pinafore dress for Christmas with a double row of large red buttons that fell where you do not want buttons to be when you are growing up. It was Royal Stuart tartan, and went down to well below my shins as I waited to 'grow into it.' I prayed at Sunday school that I would grow out of it quickly, it was so unflattering. What I wanted was a half-circular skirt with music notes on it and a waspie belt like Lorraine my older sister had, oh, and a duffel coat and fluorescent socks.

Always on New Year we had a fruit cake, and almost as much fuss was made again as our 'new mother' was from Scotland, where they know how to do things. We had Jimmy Shand and his band playing while Dad 'firstfooted' with a piece of coal - heaven only knows what that was all about.

After Christmas came the sales, often called Mammoth Sales, and I never understood that either, but Home and Fashion Stores in the Upper Precinct and British Home Stores both had bargains to sift through. Then as quick as blinking it seemed, everything disappeared, the Norway spruce, Nativity scene and all the lights, until the next year, which seems a long time when you are a child. Happy days.

Gill Yardley

Baroness Burton of Coventry

Elaine Burton was born on 2nd March 1904 in Scarborough, Yorkshire and was the daughter of Leslie and Frances Burton. Her father was an Olympic Hurdler. Elaine, at the age of sixteen was the world girls' sprint champion and she encouraged amateur sports, athletics and physical fitness, which was a life-long interest. She also played hockey for the Yorkshire First Eleven. In 1919 she was the first woman to race in shorts at the English Northern Counties Athletic Championships.

Her secondary education was completed at Lawnswood High School, Leeds. In the school magazine dated June 1936, an article was published about Elaine Burton. Many pupils could remember her as a leading light during the sports tournament and gaining many swimming honours. Her further education was carried out at Leeds City Training College.

In 1936 she was conducting Physical Training classes in an Unemployment Welfare Centre in South Wales. Before the Second World War she was a teacher, a member of the South Wales Council of Social Services, a journalist and Public Relations consultant. In 1941 she wrote a book called *What of the Women* concerning the situation of women in wartime.

Her early political experience was when she contested Hartlepool in 1943 in a by-election when she stood as a Common Wealth Party candidate. She then switched her allegiance to the Labour Party and stood for Hendon in the 1945 general election, when she was defeated. In 1950 she became the Labour MP for Coventry South; this was a newly created constituency. She scored a notable success by defeating the Conservative, Leslie Hoare Belisha, who had previously been a Liberal. He was Minister of Transport from 1934-1937 and was responsible for introducing the Belisha Beacon to mark pedestrian crossings. He was Secretary of State for War from 1937-1940. She worked alongside two other well-known Coventry Labour MPs, Richard Crossman and Maurice Edelman. In 1951 she was appointed a member of the Estimates Committee. She succeeded Mr. Sydney Silverman MP who had previously held the position. In the House of Commons she championed the feminist cause and kept an alert watch on the interests of housewife consumers and in 1955 she did a party political broadcast on behalf of the Labour Party.

When Elaine Burton heard in 1951 about complaints from the forces in Korea that they had nothing to read, she put an advertisement in a newspaper appealing for people to send books to her. She instigated 'The Book Club for Forces' and was inundated with books. On the fly-leaf they were stamped, Elaine Burton's Book Fund for Boys in Korea. Twenty-five tea chests of books were sent via the army in the U.K. to be forwarded to the soldiers in Korea.

In 1955 Elaine voted for the withdrawal of the Whip from Aneurin Bevan. She acted against the wishes of the Coventry Labour Party and the other Coventry MPs did not agree with her. She sent a detailed explanation of her action to the Coventry Labour Party in which she stated 'This has not been a matter of policy, of being Right-wing or Left-wing, but an issue of loyalty. I felt that I had no option but to give Mr. Atlee a vote of confidence'. She then sent a copy of her statement to the *Coventry Evening Telegraph*, as she felt that her constituents had the right to know why she had reached her decision. In the General Election of 1955 Coventry returned the three Labour MPs although their majorities were drastically reduced. In Elaine Burton's constituency she was only returned with a majority of 1,688 votes, compared with 5,465 in 1951. Her Conservative opponent Mrs. Murial Williamson, who contested the seat for the first time, declared 'We feel we have now brought it into the category of a marginal seat'. When the results were announced Elaine said 'I should like to thank everybody concerned in the election – the polling clerks, the counters, all the people who have contributed to the result and Mrs. Williamson for being such a good opponent'. She went on to say that she and Mrs. Williamson had not met each other until the count when they just said hello to each other. Mrs. Williamson also said 'We waved at each other earlier in the day when we were both canvassing on opposite sides of the street'. It appeared to be the general trend throughout the country with Labour's majority down.

In the General Election of 1959 Elaine Burton was defeated by Mr. Philip Hocking, a Conservative. All over the country the Conservatives had a landslide, it seems a shame that she was defeated as she worked very hard for the people of Coventry. She commented after her defeat that she did not have the faintest notion what she was going to do. She went on to say that she had been confident of retaining her seat, as the poll was much higher than before, at 85%. In her election campaign she endeavored to visit every house in the Coventry South district. When she was interviewed at her home in London, a few minutes' walk from Marble Arch, she said that she did not think that she would go on to fight another General Election. She said that firstly, of course she would have to get a job and went on to say that she had no money and it was a bit of a shock when one's income suddenly ceases. She had many letters after her defeat, not only from her friends but also from many of her political opponents. She said that for a time she would lead a quiet life and would have time for her other interests such as going to the ballet, improving her French and listening to symphonies. She also passed comment that she would miss the strenuous day with correspondence sessions in the morning and trips to the House of Commons at 2.30pm, and the frequent late sittings which she loathed. People passed comment that it would not be long before she got involved in something else, after all in the Commons she was a fighter on such issues as the Korean troops' postal charges, car hire purchase scandals and mortgage facilities for women. People said that she had not got the temperament to be dormant.

In 1959 Elaine wrote to the General Committee of Coventry South Constituency, stating that she was not going to stand for Parliament again. Her decision was regretfully received and it was proposed to hold a dinner towards the end of January when a testimonial would be presented to her. In her letter she said that her work for the city had meant a great deal, and would be pleased if some public function could be arranged to enable her to express her appreciation of the good-will she had received since she came to Coventry in 1949. Her farewell dinner was held and she was presented with a picture of herself that had been painted by Ron Morgan, (he and his wife Sonya owned the Toy Museum at Whitefriars Gate, Much Park Street, Coventry, and he later became a Coventry Councillor). The picture was behind a curtain and when she pulled the cord to reveal it; the look on her face showed that she was not pleased, as it had been painted in cubist style. I wonder what has happened to it?

In 1962 she became a life peeress along with eight other life peers; she stated that she wished to be known as Baroness Burton of Coventry, because of her connection with the city. At this time she was working at Courtaulds in the West End as a marketing consultant. Her two sponsors were Baroness

Summerskill and Baroness Wootton. She received many accolades from people stating that she always worked hard as an MP and their Lordships would hear a lot about consumer's problems. People said that she would bring a breath of fresh air to the House of Lords and display the same energy of purpose that she did in the House of Commons. As an MP, she was one of the best known women in Parliament and her dress sense once earned her the title of 'The Hon. Hat for Coventry South'. On being in the House of Lords she found that the rules forbade a peeress to speak whilst wearing her hat. She brought this matter to the notice of the House, and her recommendation was accepted and the standing order was amended, to provide for a peeress who wished, to wear a hat when speaking.

From 1962-1991, she spoke on topics including women's opportunities in business and public life and campaigned for the creation of an independent grant-supported body for sport, leading to her appointment to the newly formed Sports Council in 1965. Elaine was also appointed to the Independent Television Authority between 1964 and 1969. She left the Labour Party in 1981 to join the newly-formed Social Democratic Party. She was Opposition spokesman on civil aviation and consumer affairs and was a founder member of the National Federation of Business and Professional Women and also the Sports Council in 1965-1971.

When the Countess of Mar, then aged only 35, entered the House of Lords in 1975, Baroness Burton asked if she minded if she gave her some advice. That advice was 'specialize my dear', which she followed over the subsequent years. The Countess watched her mentor and learned by her tactics. One particular instance was when Baroness Burton stopped the airline cartels from keeping the price of flights artificially high. She fought hard to stop these cartels and won, which allowed new budget airlines like Flybe and Ryanair to come into the market. The Countess said, 'I watched how she did it' and she took a leaf out of her book when she fought campaigns herself. Once Elaine was fighting for something it was very hard to get her to change her mind. She would fight to the bitter end for the people.

There is no doubt that she worked extremely hard for the people in her constituency. It was a shame that she lost her seat in the 1959 General Election, but then throughout history people have been fickle and seem to forget the hard work that people did for them. People were electing the party and not the individual.

Elaine Burton remained unmarried and died on the 6th October 1991 at the age of 87.

Angela Atkin

Acknowledgements

My thanks to Bob Ritchie – Elaine Burton's Political Agent and also Rayanne Byatt of the History Centre for all her help.

Bibliography

Newspaper cuttings from the *Coventry Evening Telegraph* – 1951, 1955, 1959 and 1962.

A School Outing

During the summer term most schools arrange an outing for its pupils and Priory Secondary Modern School in Coventry was no exception. Form 3/1 was part of a group that travelled to London in the summer term of 1961 to visit the Tower of London, the Houses of Parliament and London Airport (Heathrow). The morning was spent at the Tower, followed by a visit to the Houses of Parliament, where we were given a guided tour by Elaine Burton, the former Coventry MP and by then Baroness Burton, when she was elevated to the House of Lords.

We arrived by coach and were directed to wait in orderly lines at an entrance, where Elaine Burton came to greet us. She was small and slim, with short, curly hair and a fairly brisk manner. She ushered us along corridors to the House of Lords, giving us information about the building and the working of the seat of government. She told us about the two chambers of the Commons and the Lords and their function in governing the country. She said we were not allowed to go into the Commons chamber, but did tell us about Black Rod and the voting system.

The chamber of the House of Lords was a large room with tiered red

86

leather benches where the Lords sat to conduct business. We were allowed to walk along the rows of benches and have a look around. She passed on more information while we were in the Lords. When it was time to leave, we followed Elaine Burton back to the door where we had entered and the coach returned to pick us up. I believe that we were only there for a short time, no longer than an hour. It was very formal and our behaviour had to be restrained.

The coach took us to London Airport where we were able to go out on the balconies with metal staircases up to the roof of the airport building. We could watch the planes taking off and landing and let off a bit of steam. There was only one terminal at the time and nowhere near as busy as it is now. In fact it seems an unusual venue to take a party of fourteen-year olds. Perhaps one of the teachers was keen on aircraft.

Lynn Hockton

Tatlow's Allesley

For more than half a century the Rainbow Inn at Allesley was known as Tatlow's Place. Over the generations the Tatlow family had been licensees. The end came when Kate Tatlow died at the age of 84 in 1958. Fortunately her granddaughter, Gill Dawkins, lives in Coventry to cherish the memories.

Kate with her granddaughter Gill.

'The Rainbow was home all through my childhood and teen years,' said Gill, a retired nurse.

'The whole family lived upstairs, grandmother, Kate, Gladys and Jack my mum and dad, and aunt, Hattie. There was a surprising amount of living accommodation, although I lived away for much of the time. Until eleven I was a weekly boarder at St. Martin's school in Solihull and then when I became a senior girl I only went home for holidays. But it was a relief to be back at The Rainbow surrounded by my family.

Summer meant hot lazy days exploring the village and fields with friends. The fields behind the church were our playground and we took picnics to the parkland of Allesley Hall.

Winter too had a special magic especially when it snowed. The gas lamps casting soft shadows on the village street; the regulars who would beat a path to the old wooden door - up the stone steps and stamping of their feet before lifting the latch; the welcoming fires in the smoke room grate; the lorries that became stuck on the slippery road outside; dad taking odd pieces of carpet and ashes out to get them going again; going up the bell tower on new year's eve and returning with the ringers to celebrate in the bottom room (now the lounge) with hot mince pies and a welcome drink.'

In common with villages up and down the country Allesley had more than its fair share of characters, none more so than the Tatlows themselves. Gill's grandmother was one.

'After grandfather died in 1931 Kate took over the licence and running of the inn with help from my parents. Kate was something of a matriarchal figure holding audiences in her special retiring room with chosen regulars. We called it "Kate's sitting room." It was next to the door from the street and she would come out to greet people just like a royal. Kate was so Victorian in her manner. She always called me "the girl" and if she saw me sitting on the settle with a leg crossed improperly she would remark "put your leg down girl."

Dad was also amazing. A real extrovert. Pictures survive with him dressed in a topper with a carnation in his lapel and a favourite pipe clasped in his left hand. He was a keen maker of home movies and he rarely went around without his cine camera at hand. He took lots of pictures of the village, the lanes, garden parties and crazy dances at the Parish Hall.

He was quite a sportsman having played hockey for England and as a cricketer, organised the Rainbow Cricket team. Often they played friendly matches with Keelavite, a factory on the way to Meriden. He even had some of the regulars batting and bowling in the car park behind the inn – soft ball of course.'

The Tatlows kept quite a menagerie behind the inn.

'There were pigs in the three large pig sties, chickens and a noisy cockerel that was always ready to peck the unwary,' said Gill. 'The occupant of the old stable was a monkey. We always had fox terriers and spaniels like Digger. He was well known in the bar and wasn't above putting his nose into a pint of beer. He had a taste for adventure and would regularly take himself to town on the bus. The police would phone up dad asking for someone to collect him. Billy the cat preferred a comfortable lookout on the window sill of the smoke room with a view of the street. He always knew when mum was fetching the meat from Mr. Harris the butcher. Billy expected some lights from her basket for supper. Another regular escapee was the tortoise. It would often make off across our garden of fruit trees, rock garden and lawn behind the inn and into the park. For some unknown reason she liked to plod across to the grounds at Allesley Hall.'

In days gone by there was often a strong relationship between the local inn and parish church. None more so than Allesley where incumbents had owned The Rainbow from the 18th century until just after the Second World War. Ownership was passed from generation to generation until the inn was sold to Atkinsons Brewery in 1949.

The Rainbow.

'We, especially my grandmother, came to know the last of the Bree family who owned the Rainbow,' Gill recalled. 'Harvey William Mapleton-Bree lived at Gable End just three properties away. After he died it passed to James Thomson Bree, an actor who lived in London. But because of the heavy death duties he had to sell up.'

The rector before the war was the Rev. Rupert Winser and Gill remembers his very large dog helping itself to cakes cooling in the open window of the kitchen. The next incumbent was also an animal lover. In the days of petrol rationing the Rev. Frank Moyle and his wife preferred a donkey and trap to trot around the village rather than a family car. Nimrod was a very smart and fastidious donkey and hated puddles. His refusal to go through them often caused mayhem in the village street but he was always ready for a juicy apple.

The churchyard itself was not without its eccentricity. While many a villager would graze their animals on the grass verge, Allesley was quite different. Gardener by name and gardener by trade, Charlie, who lived up the alley opposite in a tiny cottage, kept goats tethered in the churchyard.

Other village personalities came to the bar, a regular like Darkie who used to take the poker from a red hot fire and put it into his pint of Guinness. It made a fine hot toddy on a winter's night. Even ladies from the Stonehouse, the old people's home just a stone's throw away, came to The Rainbow.'

Gill also recalled the sight of her first banana brought in by a customer Teddy Rhodes during the war. Everyone called him Rhoda and he was like a mobile greengrocer.

'We arrived back in Allesley after the first air raids,' said Gill. 'Mother, who was pregnant with me, had been evacuated to the Old Rectory (now a private house) in Rushden, Northamptonshire away from an industrial city. The cellar where generations of villagers had staged cock fighting, was now a refuge for us when the sirens sounded. The village school was heavily sandbagged and used as a first aid post and farther up the village street was a guest house – Park Lodge – where American servicemen were billeted. They used to come into The Rainbow for a drink.'

After the years at The Rainbow, Gill Tatlow had an immensely varied career that started at the well-known secretarial school – Underwoods. While she enjoyed developing typing skills, her ability to learn shorthand was less than good and it was soon time to find a new career.

'I had to move on and was lucky enough to get an apprenticeship in a hairdressing salon in Keresley called Audrey Fielding. I served my five years there and then moved to another hairdresser's in Styvechale – Rosettas. But I was still far from happy with my career.

It was the late 1950s and the golden age of car making in Coventry, and having passed my driving test I was attracted to the job of a professional driver in the motor industry. In those days car delivery was common practice and drivers had their own trade plates. I found work at Mortons Car Deliveries and was put onto driving new cars all over the area – they were the days of Heralds, TR3's and Spitfire sports cars, even the powerful Sunbeam Tigers and the like.

However, there would still be another twist in my life as I had always wanted to work abroad. It was something of a shot in the dark when I found work as an extra with a film company in Barcelona. The film involved a circus from Germany and was called "Circus World." Just imagine me working with some of the big names – John Wayne, Rita Hayworth and Claudia Cardinali.

When I came home the call of the road returned immediately and not surprisingly I found work with another car delivery firm – Nobles of Croft Road. Driving every type of Jaguar all over the country really was a crowning experience but the E Type was my favourite.'

In 1966 Gill Tatlow married at Meriden Parish Church and became a housewife for the first time in her life. These days she enjoys working with young people at the 8F Squadron (1st City of Coventry) Air Training Corps. But her first love is motoring on the open road in her classic Mini Cooper. With her husband Martin they founded the Central Mini Owners' Club.

Elizabeth Draper

Acknowledgements

With thanks to Gill Dawkins

Betty Saltiel

Betty Saltiel died in October 2006, at the age of 77, her family, friends, former colleagues and pupils decided to gather together, in the December, to pay tribute to her life and achievements. The memorial meeting was held at John Gulson School in George Street where Betty taught in the 1960s, 70s and 80s. Betty a committed teacher, also taught at Alderman's Green and Longford Park Schools and following her retirement continued to work as a supply teacher in many schools across the city. This was quite an unusual event for someone who was proud to have started and ended their career as a classroom teacher.

Shaukat Hussain, the present Head of John Gulson School said 'I am delighted to be hosting this event. Betty was a very popular teacher at the school and continued to keep in touch. She attended our 50th Anniversary in 2006 and was always interested in what was happening here.'

Andy Walmsley, who at the time was co-ordinating the Coventry Excellence in Schools programme and head of Longford Park during her time there, said 'Betty had a genuine liking for all the youngsters and a real interest in their learning. She taught from the heart. Her pupils and their parents genuinely liked her.'

At the memorial event previous pupils spoke of what they felt they owed to Betty. Mark Hall spoke of her as being 'inspirational, I wouldn't be here now if it wasn't for Betty Saltiel. She would tell us stories of her and her husband Henry's beginnings in a deprived area of London and would always encourage us to aspire. She would say "you can be anything you want to be." Mark went on to Sidney Stringer Comprehensive School and then to study law at university. He was successful and is very clear that he and others owe some of their success to Betty. Betty's friend and colleague at John Gulson, Brenda Hillier, spoke of Betty as 'a fantastic teacher' and how 'Betty valued every single child. Betty was a great advocate for children and very keen to promote gender equality, for example, encouraging boys to learn needlework.' This was at a time when the school was taking in more and more minority ethnic pupils, a part of her work Betty really enjoyed. 'The children loved her – she got them all involved and she encouraged discussions at "circle time" long before it became accepted practise. Her classroom was somehow always different; brighter than others and always had the children's work on display. Above all her skill as a story teller was incredible – telling tales of her early life, especially during the war years, that brought it to life and which they found fascinating.' Another colleague spoke of when they took the children away to Southam for an activity holiday. 'The children absolutely adored her.' She also remembers 'Betty and the bananas. We had been given these bananas by a father who worked at Barras Heath Market but needed to use them quickly because they were turning black in places. Betty immediately took over with "that's no problem you just bake them with sugar;" which she did. The problem was that the combination of the bananas and sugar seemed to produce an alcoholic pudding. The children slept really well that night.'

Sandra Shipton, another colleague and long-time friend spoke of Betty as an active trade unionist and a member of the National Union of Teachers (NUT). She was a member of the Executive group and attended many of the sub-committees; especially the gender and, when formed later, the anti-racist sub-committee. She became President of Coventry Association in 1989 at a time when many changes were taking place. She was a regular attendee at the national conference and would always be there to speak either in favour or against proposed motions. Sandra was often at conference with Betty and she remembers Betty's fierce support of the classroom teacher. Sandra speaks of Betty's ideas as 'being before her time.' Betty often said 'we shouldn't have to leave the classroom to receive extra remuneration for doing a good job.' Later the Government recognised this sentiment and decided to reward those who chose to stay in the classroom rather than go into management.

As part of the Gender sub-committee she took part in the seminal research undertaken by Coventry NUT in 1984. The Coventry Association was keen to identify the position of women teachers and the barriers to promotion that they were experiencing. As a result the local Education Authority set up its own working party and appointed an Equal Opportunities Advisor to examine what was happening within the Authority and to implement policies to bring about change. Sandra, who had led the research programme, said 'Betty was always socially and politically active and continued to be involved in a variety of organisations until her death. While well into her 70s she went on a computer course to enable her to keep up with technology. This was unique for a woman of her age to have still been so heavily involved in political life for such a long time.'

Betty was also elected as the Primary School Representative on Coventry's Education Committee where she was able to promote the work of teachers and support policies that enhanced the lives of both teachers and pupils.

Tim Healey, Project Director for Coventry's Better Government for Older People (BGOP), gave us a view of Betty 'in retirement'.

'When Betty "retired" everyone who knew her realised that this related to her work and not from activism.

Betty became very involved with the Trades Council offshoot – The British Pensioners and Trades Union Action Association – Coventry 4:20 led by the, till then at least, indomitable Jack Sprung. It soon became clear that no town was going to be big enough for both of these reconstructed Marxist firebrands and Betty along with Jack Gould decided to concentrate on forming the Coventry Older People's Forum in order to pursue a broader rights agenda.

Not long after, a callow young man at the council – me – became Project Director of BGOP with the publicised priority of establishing "a forum for older people in Coventry." As those who knew her could testify, it was no surprise when Betty got in touch! Imagine if you would the phone call….. "Is that Mr Healey, are you the man who's going to set up a forum for older people in Coventry? RIGHT MATE…………"

This was the start of a fabulous, tumultuous, cathartic, dramatic, high energy working relationship which, if I live to retire as a local government officer at the (by then) age of 75, I'll be very lucky to see the likes again.

In the bright new dawn days of 1997 with "things can only get better" still ringing in our ears, I was approached by central government who were seeking nominated delegates from BGOP pilot areas. They were looking for intelligent, articulate but passionate advocates for older people to sit around the table with a range of Government Ministers to put the case for older people. In my case the nomination was easy and Betty soon became a fixture in the no- longer-smoke filled rooms of darkest Whitehall.

Many great things happened as a result of this:
Winter Fuel Payments for Older People;
Free TV licenses for over 75s;
Anti-Discrimination legislation on age;
Linking of pensions to earnings;
Radical new health care standards.

All of this radical change came as a result of that initial People's Advisory Group (OPAG) work.

Betty, God love her, fared less well once democracy took over from hand-picking as a way of selecting members of OPAG and when popularity amongst the electorate was going to hold sway, we all new that Betty's pugnacious, take no prisoners style was going to count against her. She never got elected to OPAG's national committee but I feel it is absolutely true to say that this was to its detriment and the progress made in the six months at the beginning with Betty on board has never been replicated.

A highlight of this period for Betty was her being a delegate at an International Colloquy of older people in Prague in 1999. Betty led the UK delegation's presentation to the assembled representatives of older people from around the world. She read out the much re-read poem by Benjamin Zephaniah – WE – to a rapturous reception. I wasn't there, but Betty told me she was fantastic! I'm sure she was. Betty was later very proud to have the poem signed by Zephaniah. It was a prized possession.

There are few people I can name that have had a real impact on the lives of millions of people – but Betty is certainly one such – and I like to think if I ever retire, my life, and everyone else's will be better because of her.'

So who was Betty? What were her origins? What made her the activist she became?

She was born Betty Davis in Stepney, London in 1929 into an Orthodox Jewish family. Her father was a taxi driver. This was the time of the 'Great Depression' and she was aware at a young age of poverty and deprivation which was all around her and spoke of her mother pretending they had something to eat in the pot but in truth it was only a thin broth. Politics surrounded her and she spoke of seeing 'the Black shirts led by their leader, the fascist Oswald Mosley, marching through her area of London, where many Jewish people lived.' Betty spoke with pride of the time she and her cousin, Marie, acting as 'spies,' crept into a group meeting of the Fascist organisation. They listened carefully and then reported back to her family. Given she was only 10 years old when the war started this was an impressive act.

Betty's parents were very aware of what was happening in Germany and were active in the Kinder-transport movement offering a home to Jewish children whose parents sent them abroad to escape the Nazi persecution. Later in her life, when Betty had settled in Coventry, she also offered a home to Chilean refugees escaping the persecution of General Pinochet's regime. They lived with her for some time and remained friends until her death.

Although the world around her was presenting troubled times Betty discovered her love for the cinema and the theatre, to which her parents took her, when they could afford it. For the rest of her life she would be an avid devotee of the cinema. What was amazing was her absolutely phenomenal memory. She knew every film that she had seen; which cinema it had been shown at; who she had gone with; the story and all the major players. With this memory she enhanced her skills as a vivid teller of history who kept the oral tradition alive.

I will gloss over her life during the Second World War as when Betty was part of this Women's Research Group she wrote an extraordinary tale of her family's experiences of the evacuation of children to safer areas. (See this account in *Making the Best of Things* 2007)

After the war Betty went out to work and tried out several areas. One of these was a cigarette factory and probably where Betty started smoking. She also trained as, or worked with, a chiropodist at some point although does not appear to have taken this up.

Betty also joined the Unity Theatre group that was eventually to lead to a meeting with the man who became her husband and who she described as 'having a warmth and exuberance that was difficult to convey' and with whom she lived, until his death in 1980. Their paths must have crossed several times as Henry was also born in Stepney some three years before

Betty. She wrote 'Henry moved to Sigdon Road in Stepney and in 1936, I was living in flats called Evelyn Court, exactly opposite for some two years. We may have walked along the road to school at the same time each day as Sigdon Road was my Primary School.' Unity Theatre was also to be a link between them. Betty again wrote 'Once I was sixteen my parents began to take me to see productions and I continued to see occasional plays. I joined the local Unity group in Hackney and even went on two summer schools organised by the leader who ran our group.' Henry was by then a regular attendee and performer. 'He had discovered the Unity Theatre through his socialist work colleagues who he worked alongside with in a Marconi factory doing essential war-work. They also helped him to form his thinking about his religious beliefs and his political development.' Unity Theatre was formed in the mid-thirties as the first left wing theatre in this country. It began as street performance until it acquired a derelict chapel between Kings Cross and Camden.

It was 1951 before Betty and Henry finally met. Their friendship developed during a Unity Theatre visit to the German Democratic Republic (GDR). The Theatre toured the GDR and after three weeks they realised that they were in love with each other, and on a wet November day were married at Bevis Marks Synagogue in London.

Henry had been training as an optician but was unhappy and so returned to factory life where he was amongst fellow workers from the communist and other socialist parties. At some point Betty and Henry became committed members of the Communist Party. However, in later years she referred to herself as a socialist and not a communist.

Henry saw himself as an actor but both he and Betty were pragmatists realising that it was too precarious a profession. Henry had always been concerned about education and had a deep rooted respect for children; they discussed the possibility of Henry becoming a teacher. Betty said that their first real date had been going to a meeting about changes in post-war education! Henry applied for and was accepted at a local College of Education but had to take a loan out to pay for his training. Money was a real issue. Betty was pregnant with her first child so had to give up her work. It was only with family support; Henry working high days and holidays and by Betty going back to work as a temporary secretary when their son,

David, was one year old, did they manage to get through.

Betty and Henry continued to be members of the Unity Theatre: it was a large part of their lives. Betty helped behind the scenes working on productions and in the office. They were still living in Hackney, in what Betty described as a 'grotty flat with a shared lavatory, no bathroom, minute kitchen and two rooms.' They decided to try for a house in the Harlow New Town. Henry managed to get a job at a local school and they moved there with their sons, David and Mark in 1956.

At the same time Betty had not given up on her political activism. A firm believer in the Campaign for Nuclear Disarmament she was a regular protester on many rallies pushing Mark in his pushchair and David walking alongside or borne aloft by Henry. Betty would continue marching and protesting against injustice for the rest of her life. I remember the protest march against Apartheid held in London in July 1988. Betty, myself and friends were on our way for a six week visit to Ghana, but first we joined the march and were fortunate to hear Desmond Tutu speak. My abiding memory was, however, being on a bus and finding that Tony Benn was a fellow passenger. We were a group that admired his principles and Betty decided that she could not let the opportunity pass to say something to him. I must admit to my surprise, because what she said was so simple but so important. After apologising for disturbing him she said, 'thank you for all your efforts on our behalf, we appreciate all you do. Carry on the good work.' More recently Betty and a few friends, who were unable to go to London to join the march against the invasion of Iraq, started their own group – Coventry against the War. On the day of the London march hundreds of people marched around Coventry to show their solidarity led by Betty and her friends.

Due to a promotion for Henry the family moved to Dunstable where Betty decided to also train as a teacher. She chose to train in the Foebel technique, which although originally for kindergarten had been shown to translate successfully to older pupils.

Betty arrived in Coventry in 1968 having come with Henry to his new position as a Lecturer in Education at, what was then, Canley Teacher Training College. They moved into Cecily Road in Cheylesmore and the two boys went to Whitley Abbey School, while Betty settled in at John Gulson

Primary School. She was lucky to find a group of teachers who held the same philosophical beliefs as herself especially on education; Community Education alongside multi-cultural education was beginning in some of the inner city schools. John Gulson was one school that was open to new ideas and everyone pulled together to ensure that pupils achieved to the best of their ability.

Betty lived and worked through a period of immense change. In 1976 after the successful socialist revolution in Mozambique, Betty and Henry decided to visit and offer their skills to this emerging country. They enjoyed their time there and Betty was particularly proud to have met the President. Unfortunately Henry became ill and they had to return after only one year. Henry died three years later, in 1980, causing a gaping hole in Betty's life. He had not just been a husband but a true soul mate with whom no one could compare. However, with the tenacity we had come to expect, Betty threw herself into her teaching and the many causes dear to her heart.

Betty spent her time in Coventry working for its children and teachers but she always found time for others. She was a member of the Samaritans, which surprised many people including myself; that formidable façade could be gentle when dealing with those in need. She became a Trustee for the Sahara Project; a unique project set up specifically to explore and provide culturally appropriate support to meet the needs of Asian older people with mental health difficulties. Above all as another friend said; she was a really good friend illustrating this by saying, 'I was going through a painful divorce and desperately needed someone to talk to so I phoned Betty at 1am. Betty immediately said, "I'll be with you in a few minutes," and sure enough she soon appeared with a bottle of brandy and a packet of 'fags'!'

During her final years Betty became very interested in the background of the Saltiel* family group to which Henry would have belonged. In 1994 there had been a conference in the Netherlands. To the surprise of many, people came from around the world. Many had thought that they were the only Saltiels surviving. In 2009 they had identified some 2,500 people and the figure was growing. Betty attended the conference and also one held in Salamanca in 1997. She made new 'family' friends and also wrote a biography of Henry for the *Shealtiel Gazette*; 'the international medium of communication between members of the family,' from which I have used 'her voice' for information and comments throughout this piece.

Everyone who met Betty has their own story to tell. Betty, in her spare time, was also very skilled at needlecraft and found time to make many things, but especially in later years she began to make quilts. To end this short biography I have included this piece written by Lynn Hockton. I think this is very appropriate as it speaks of Betty at the time of her death. Lynn writes:

'I first met Betty when I joined the Saturday afternoon group of Shire Quilters. I got to know her on a trip the Quilters Guild organised to the Isle of Man in 2003. During the long weekend Betty had a nasty fall and broke her shoulder. On the plane home we sat together and once

Betty Saltiel.

home I went around to see if she needed help with shopping, etc., we then became close friends and enjoyed sitting and talking while getting on with our sewing.

We set up a small group of retired women in Canley, making patchwork tops, which Betty and I turned into Linus Quilts. These were given to hospitals, hospices and the Fire Service for distribution to children who were terminally ill or traumatised in some way. We made over one hundred brightly coloured quilts until the group gradually ceased.

Betty belonged to a group called What Older Women Want (WOWW) and I belonged to the Women's Research Group. Both groups were short of members so we suggested to our respective groups that we attend the others' meetings to boost numbers, but to keep the ethos of each group separate. This worked very successfully until Betty's death, when WOWW closed. The remaining funds in the kitty paid for a silver cup in Betty's name that was presented to John Gulson School.

When Betty became ill in 2006 the decline was quite rapid. She recovered from a cataract operation quite well but she then seemed to slow down and in July was taken into hospital with heart problems. Once she came out she never regained her health and strength and found it difficult to walk any distance. She had another stay in hospital in the September but at the beginning of October while using a new adjustable bed she fell out and broke her hip. She was found the next morning by a friend and rushed to hospital. Whilst being put in the ambulance Betty managed a joke with her friend "well at least I've managed to bring the Earlsdon traffic to a stand-still." Because of Betty's heart condition they could not operate until she was stabilized. Her sons came from Yorkshire and were at her bedside when I visited her a few days later. She died less than one week after her fall.

Betty's sons asked if I would help to clear all her quilting things and we decided to sell them at Shire Quilters and the money raised should go to Cancer Research, a charity close to Betty's heart. I realised there was the making of several quilts that Betty had prepared and planned and I decided that I would make up the potential quilts myself and give at least one each to her sons and the friends who had helped her so much. It was my way of dealing with the grief I felt at Betty's death. Over the next twelve months I made eleven quilts from Betty's stash. Two each for her sons, one each for Jeannie, Sandra, Brenda and her cousin Marie and I kept three for myself. It brought tears to the eyes of more than one recipient of these quilts to have a memento of Betty.

The sale at Shire Quilters made £100 for Cancer Research. Whenever I use the pieces that I bought at the sale, I think of Betty and know she would be pleased to think her possessions have been used and were giving pleasure to those that received them.'

I think a fitting tribute to Betty would be 'those that knew her will not forget her.'

Janice Wale

Acknowledgements

Thanks to all those who contributed to this article: Tim Healey, Brenda Hillier, Lynn Hockton, Sandra Shipton and others who passed on information. Where I have quoted Betty this is mainly from the *Sheatiel Gazette Vol:2*, 1996. My thanks go to the editor for allowing its inclusion here.

Thank you to Coventry City Council for permission to reproduce the photograph of Betty.

*Saltiel can be spelt in a number of ways.

Della Bowen – A Very Special Person

Della Bowen was born in Galway on 10th January 1915. She lost both her parents at an early age and was brought up by her grandmother. She spent her early formative years in Ireland. Her grandmother lived in a railway cottage and it was Della's job to open and shut the gates for the passing trains. This cottage is still lived in by Della's youngest sister although the gates are now operated by electricity. Della had three sisters, Theresa, who died after Della, Mary, and Jennie who still lives in the railway cottage in Galway.

In 1934, at the age of 19, Della decided to leave her native Ireland. She arrived in Coventry and obtained a job at the GEC. She met her future husband Jim who worked on the track at Rootes. They married in 1936 and made their home in Tennyson Road, Coventry where they raised their family of Malcolm, Georgina and Randall. She was married to Jim for 56 years until his death in 1992. Her sister, Mary, also followed her to Coventry, and is still living in the city. In 1986, Della planned a party for her family and friends to celebrate her Golden Wedding. She went to the bank on Ball Hill, Coventry to draw out money to pay for the party. Unfortunately a youth saw her take the money from the cashier and as she was walking home he grabbed her bag, knocking her to the ground. Della would not cancel the party so her photographs of the event show her with a black eye.

Golden Wedding Celebration.

Della and the family were regular churchgoers and attended Mass at Sacred Heart Catholic Church in Stoke, throughout the years of the 2nd World War. In 1946 Della was invited to join the Union of Catholic Mothers where she became a very enthusiastic and active member for the next 50 years. During this time she held nearly every office at the branch and

Archdiocesan level, culminating in her being elected as President of the Archdiocese for the years 1985 to 1988.

During her work with the Mothers Union, Della had developed an interest in people with disabilities and took a job as a cleaner at Burns Road Occupational Centre which was very near to her house in Tennyson Road. It was this interest which led her daughter, Georgie, to become interested in disabled children and to become the first trainee teacher in Coventry for disabled children. Della was a fountain of knowledge and helped parents and disabled people in many ways giving practical advice. As her family were now older, she took a job as Care Assistant at Broad Park Care Home in Henley Green in 1954. This was a short stay respite home for children with severe learning difficulties. She worked there for 20 years until her retirement, by which time she had risen to the position of Head of the Home. However, her passion for the children with severe learning difficulties extended beyond her job and she continued to work for many years after retirement.

In 1958 she helped to found the Catholic Handicapped Fellowship, where she became the Secretary and held this post for 40 years until a few years before she died. The fellowship was to play a major part in her life and to take up a considerable amount of her time. She was involved in organising fund raising events, visiting and supporting the families of disabled children in the Coventry area, arranging monthly Masses and Discos, as well as various parties throughout the year.

However, one of the highlights of the Fellowship for Della was the annual Easter Pilgrimage to the holy site of Lourdes in France with the St Bernadette's Trust. Della would regularly take upwards of a dozen children and adults with disabilities

Della on one of the pilgrimages to Lourdes.

105

to Lourdes accompanied by her loyal and enthusiastic group of helpers. Della would always arrive each year with numerous large cardboard boxes containing endless varieties of breakfast cereals, crisps and chocolates, together with a number of large containers of orange cordial so that her charges would not be denied their creature comforts while in France. Altogether she made 22 pilgrimages with the Trust, only missing out in 1992 when her husband died and in 2005 when the doctors would not allow her to travel. She also went to Lourdes over 40 times with the Sue Ryder Trust. This meant that she was involved in taking sick people to Lourdes on 63 occasions in her life-time.

The other special event in Della's year was the two week holiday for the Handicapped Fellowship group to Barmouth. She and her band of helpers would take 22 to 25 disabled persons for a holiday each year in order to give their parents and carers a break. These holidays were an annual event for 28 years until 2005. It was Della's wish that these holidays should continue in future and her family and friends have set up a charitable fund to finance them.

Della's selfless devotion to others had been recognised by various awards and commendations. The one of which she was most proud of was the Papal award of the Bene Merenti in recognition of her work with the Union of Catholic Mothers. This was presented to her by Pope John Paul II when he visited Coventry in 1986. She was also Coventry's Woman of the year in 1985, Irish Woman of the Year in 1993, Coventry Irish Person of the Year in 2001. She received the Pro Ecclesia Medal in 1986 for 30 years work with the Catholic Handicapped Fellowship and the Heart of Britain 1994.

On her 90th birthday she wanted to celebrate the occasion by having a huge party. As she pointed out to her family she wanted to have a celebration as she would not be there at her Wake! The day started with a special mass for her at St John Fisher's Church. She was amazed to find a plush limousine waiting for her outside the church with champagne, waiting to whisk her off to a special birthday lunch. A party was arranged for 150 family and friends and her relatives from her home city of Galway were among the guests. She received letters and commendations from the Irish Premier Bertie Ahern and from the Irish President Mary McAleese. She asked for donations to the Catholic Association for Overseas Development instead of presents as she had been hugely touched by the Asian tsunami at the time. An amount of £1800 was donated to help the victims and she was very proud of this amount raised. In November 2005 she was nominated for the Coventry Local Hero award.

Della had a long happy and very active life, mostly devoted to helping others. This is reflected in the various comments made about her, for example:

'She is second to none. She is a fantastic, precious and kind person who has taken my boys to Lourdes for 30 years.'

'I think of her as my second Mum. She is always there for you whether you want to laugh or cry.'

'I have been on trips with Della for over 30 years and I don't know what I'd do without her.'

'She has been helpful with my son for many years and is always there for support. No matter what a person needs, she will be there to help.'

Everyone she came into contact with knew her as an extremely kind, caring and considerate person who was always willing to help others in any way possible. She was an amazing lady, who touched the hearts of so many people; in fact she was one of those people of whom you could truly say she is irreplaceable.

Ann Waugh

Acknowledgements

Thank you to Georgie Larsen-Archer.

Pam Rossiter

Although not originally from Coventry, Pam came to the city on the first of June 1962, a week after the consecration of the new cathedral. Originally Pam lived in a flat in Charter Avenue, but then moved to Astill Grove and later to Earlsdon.

Pam worked as a Social Worker in Coventry. She initially worked in the children's department run by Miss Mary Barnes* who was the Children's Officer. It was a social work organisation but the Social Workers did not have the whole range of work as they do now, instead it was just concerned with children in care or those children who were at risk of going into care.

At that time Social Workers in Coventry were split into two sections. Originally Pam worked in the north team, but later moved over to the south team and worked her way up until she became the most senior person in the team. Pam's role included management of the south team. She worked mainly with children who were already in care, especially the children in the many small children's homes. She also had the responsibility of ensuring the care of children placed in these homes, was adequate.

Although a difficult job to do, it was a job Pam was trained for and already had quite a lot of experience in before she came to Coventry. Pam had been in the WRENS but left to study social science at Bristol University. After qualification she worked in Newport, Huntingdon and Birmingham before Coventry. She explained that at that time you could move around between local authorities without too much difficulty, or change jobs. Pam stated that although difficult at times she never regretted her choice of career, even at a time when women were expected to become teachers or nurses. She described how she could not imagine doing anything else or enjoying anything else as much, and it was a good life in many ways.

Pam talked about working in the Social Work Team. Each member of the team specialised a little in different areas of work, from working with families to working with people who had mental health difficulties. Overall it was a bit of a hotchpotch as everyone dealt with everybody, and did this in the best way that they could. She described how training to be a social worker was different to now and people came through many different routes into social work. A major difference was that back then some people did not have a professional qualification. Pam explained how the whole social work team were keen to help, but they did not always know the right way to go about it. Pam talked about one member of the team who was quite wealthy. He used to give people money to help them. Pam considered this as highly unprofessional and not at all the sort of thing that was helpful to the department or anybody else. However, without professional training in social work people were unsure how to help and just did the best they could.

Pam reflected on the modern role of a Social Worker and how the role had changed so much that she would not touch it with a barge pole! She believes Social Workers now have to live with their heads looking over their shoulders all the time. In the past they had a much freer role where the team could work in a way they felt was appropriate. Pam talked about how this sense of freedom resulted in better work as people were not worried about being penalised for making a small mistake. There was no 'come back' in the early days and Pam described how at the end of the day you could shut the office door and not worry about work until the next day. There certainly was not the constant fear, as there is now, that you could be taken to court for doing your job.

Pam settled in Coventry and got to know the city pretty well. In 1977 she married the Deputy City Architect in the cathedral. Pam and Basil married by special licence as they did not want the publicity that would come from having the marriage banns read.

Pam and her husband Basil were both 51 when they were married. Her husband had spent a long time telling everyone he was a confirmed bachelor, so they married rather quietly, with very few people present in the cathedral's Lady Chapel, and shot off on honeymoon until everybody got over the shock of the wedding. However, the wedding did not remain a quiet affair for long; the couple had their photograph taken by the local newspaper and it became headline news, ending up on the front cover of the *Coventry Evening Telegraph*. Pam said that it was quite a 'hoo haa' at the time but when they returned from honeymoon on the Monday morning most people had 'sort of got used to the idea.'

Both Pam and Basil were amazed to discover that not only were they both from Wiltshire, but were also both born in Devizes in Wiltshire within a couple of months of each other and in the same nursing home. Pam explained that this is why they got along so well as 'they had so much in common.' She found when they actually got together that 'it was all a bit strange.' They met when they both attended a concert at the cathedral. Pam was alone and sat with Basil as she recognised him from the cathedral. They started talking initially about the cathedral and then about themselves and found out they had a lot in common and were intellectually very close, enjoying many of the same interests. Pam related how she got on so well with Basil that she asked him if he wanted to talk to her mother who was also from Devizes and would love to talk about the area. She invited Basil to lunch on the following Sunday and describes this as the 'beginning of the whole saga.' Pam remembers that following their wedding her mother said 'You have married a funny man, Pam,' and that she was not sure if she really meant it as funny ha ha or funny peculiar either!

Pam worked for another six years after she married before taking redundancy. She explained how the Social Work team was being reorganised and she did not want to go through the process again. Nowadays, Pam is a regular worshipper at Coventry Cathedral and it is a big part of her life. She stressed how much she enjoyed being a part of a friendly church and also being part of the reconciliation ministry. This ministry stems back to Provost Howard, one of the cathedral provosts at the time of the bombing of the old cathedral on 14th November 1940. Provost Howard wrote 'Father Forgive' in the old cathedral and stressed that this meant that we all needed to be forgiven. Over time this became the reconciliation ministry and the 'Litany of Reconciliation' is said every weekday at the Cathedral, and also by all the 'cross of nails' centres of which there are over 600, based all over the world.

Pam is a member of the Cathedral Welcome Team, which as the name suggests welcomes new worshippers and visitors to the cathedral. Pam described how she is always willing to share her vast knowledge of the cathedral with other people.

Pam is a keen member of The National Trust and is also a Soroptimist. Together Soroptimist groups form Soroptimist International. This is a worldwide service organisation for women. It is dedicated to helping women and girls to achieve both their individual and collective potential, to realise their aspirations and have an equal say in the development of strong, peaceful communities all over the world.

Although she does not describe herself as a Coventrian, as she was not born in the city, Pam has enjoyed her time in Coventry and met some wonderful characters.

Ali McGarry

Thank you to Pam for sharing her memories.
*See our publication *Redressing the Balance*

Mo Mowlam

Marjorie Mowlam was born in Watford on 18th September 1949, the second of three children of Tina and Frank Mowlam. She was educated at Chiswick Girl's grammar school in West London.

The family later moved to Coventry and lived in Styvechale Avenue, Earlsdon. Mo, as she liked to be called, attended Coundon Court Comprehensive School where she became head girl. (This was previously the home of George Singer the car manufacturer). She became interested in politics at an early age, but she had thought of becoming a doctor, as she felt their work was practical and got results.

Her father Frank became Coventry's assistant postmaster. Unfortunately, he was an alcoholic and she would never take any of her friends home, as she never knew what state her father would be in. When she came in from school she would go upstairs to do her homework, possibly to stay out of her father's way. Her mother Tina, worked as a telephone supervisor at Owen Owen, a department store, situated in Broadgate (now Primark). Tina worked to help supplement the family's income and was a strong and determined woman.

Mo first had her name printed in the *Coventry Evening Telegraph* in March 1965 along with two school friends, when they offered to give the Lady Godiva statue a much needed wash and brush-up. The authorities turned down their offer on health and safety grounds. The statue on its plinth is 18 foot high and it would have needed two ladders.

When she left school she went to Trevelyan College at Durham University to obtain a degree in Anthropology and Sociology. During her first year she joined the Labour Party and later worked in London for Tony Benn, the Labour MP and as a research assistant for an American writer Alvin Toffler. The staff at Durham were not happy about Mo's student room one summer because of all the Jimi Hendrix posters stuck on the walls and they had difficulty in letting it during the summer. Following her graduation from Durham in 1973 Mo moved to America where she completed a PhD in Political Science at the University of Iowa. In 1977 she lectured briefly in politics at both the University of Wisconsin and Florida State University.

She returned to England in 1979, accepting a position to lecture in Politics at the University of Newcastle-upon-Tyne. At this time she also worked in adult education at Northern College, Barnsley, with students who had fewer opportunities than many university students had. She arranged a series of alternative lectures that were published as *Debate and Disarmament* in 1981, which she jointly edited. The proceeds from the book went to the Campaign for Nuclear Disarmament.

Politics was Mo's passion and she had been a member of the Labour Party since 1969. In 1987 she was elected Labour MP for Redcar, North Yorkshire. She held this position for fourteen years until 2001. She was very popular with the electorate, as she was a bit of a charmer, with an easy going nature and a sense of humour. She later became a member of the influential House of Commons Public Accounts Committee and the party's ruling National Executive Committee. In 1994 she helped to organise Tony Blair's leadership bid. He described her as 'one of the most remarkable and colourful personalities ever to enter British politics'. Blair appointed her Shadow Secretary of State for Northern Ireland. This was regarded as the toughest job in Britain and over the next few years she held various other opposition posts.

In 1995, at the age of 46 she married Jon Norton, a merchant banker. He had two children from his previous marriage and she became stepmother to Henrietta and Freddie who she loved very much.

A few weeks before the May 1997 general election, Mo was diagnosed with a brain tumour and had to have radiotherapy and steroid treatment. As a result she gained weight, although people thought it was because she had given up smoking. She suffered hair loss and had to wear a wig, but soon abandoned this even though she had thinning hair. Her surgeon wanted to operate on the tumour but Mo did not want this, as she was determined to achieve a high position in parliament. In fact she did not even tell her mother sister or brother about the tumour. One person she told about her illness was Nigel, her political adviser. The other person she told was Tony Blair but she told him that she had been diagnosed with a benign brain tumour and that she was having radiotherapy and coping well and that everything was under control and was not a problem.

When Labour won the 1997 election, she was appointed Secretary of State for Northern Ireland and later that year was admitted to the Privy

Council for Northern Ireland. Her main task was to find a peaceful solution to the troubles in Northern Ireland.

Mo set about working towards the restoration of an IRA ceasefire, her illness did little to dent her determination to get the two sides talking. In 1998 she decided that she would visit the Maze Prison near Belfast, to speak to both loyalist and republican prisoners face-to-face. She knew that an IRA ceasefire could only go forward if Sinn Fein the political wing or the IRA, was represented in the peace process. Sinn Fein's involvement was blocked by suspicious loyalist political prisoners who were still able to control outside events from their cells. Within two hours of her visit to the prison Sinn Fein announced it was being allowed to rejoin the talks. Shortly after, the Good Friday Agreement for Ireland was secured on 10th April 1998.

In 1998, Mo's handling of the controversial Orange Order parade through a mainly Catholic area to Drumcree was one of her lowest moments. The residents said that she had promised to let them know in advance whether she would allow the parade to proceed. But in the end the police and army moved in without warning and allowed the parade to go ahead.

Also in 1998, in response to a special request by Tony Blair, Elton John performed an open-air concert at Stormont. Mo welcomed the concert saying that she wanted to open Stormont Castle facilities to the public. Elton John gave his services free. Profits from the £25 a head tickets were going to be used towards building education facilities in the castle's parkland. The idea of the concert was to bring together young people from both sides of the conflict.

During that year Mo was offered the Freedom of the City of Coventry, a great privilege offered to very few. She was also given an Honorary Doctorate by Coventry University. She came to the city to receive these honours.

Mo was replaced as Northern Ireland Secretary by Peter Mandelson in 1999. She was widely praised by Catholic parties, especially the Social Democratic and Labour Party (SDLP). The Irish Prime Minister, Bertie Ahern, praised her for her courage and understanding. The Unionists were less sorry to see her go. Many of them believed she was biased in favour of Sinn Fein. They disapproved of her visit to the Maze Prison and her tendency to come across as much more touchy-feely than any other holder of the post. Well she was the first woman to hold this position! David Trimble made no comment about her leaving, she never saw eye to eye with him. Ian Paisley passed the comment that she was a failure. Mo returned to London as Cabinet Minister, in charge of co-ordinating and promoting government policies, she was also responsible for the government's stance on drugs. She caused some controversy when she attracted media attention after admitting to having used cannabis as a student, she said 'I tried dope. I did not particularly like it'. She held this office, but was disenchanted with Tony Blair's leadership and was a vocal opponent of the war in Iraq. On the 4th September 2000 she announced her intention to retire from Parliament and finally stepped down as an MP at the General Election of June 2001. She was sorely missed by the people of Redcar.

After her retirement from the House of Commons she became a noted critic of government policy on various issues, especially Iraq. She set up a charity, MoMo Helps, to help drug users who were successfully completing their rehabilitation and to provide support for the parents and carers of disabled children.

On the 3rd August 2005, it was reported that she was critically ill at King's College Hospital, London. She appeared to have suffered from balance problems due to the effects of the tumour. According to her husband she fell over and received head injuries and never regained consciousness. She had made a living will in which she asked not to be resuscitated and food and water were withdrawn. On the 12th August 2005, she was moved to Pilgrims Hospice, Kent, where she died seven days later at the age of 55. Mo was an atheist and was cremated at Sittingbourne, Kent on 1st September 2005. Following a non-religious service half of her ashes were scattered at Hillsborough Castle, the Secretary of State for Northern Ireland's official residence, the other half in her former parliamentary constituency of Redcar. Her funeral was a quiet family affair. Two memorial services were held for her. The first on 20th November 2005 at The Theatre Royal in Drury Lane, London and the second on 3rd December 2005 in Redcar.

Mo Mowlam will be remembered for her toughness and courage, as well as her persistence and good humour. She was affable and straightforward and was able to talk to anyone. She gained an enormous amount of public popularity and support for her work in Northern Ireland by handling one of the most dangerous and challenging jobs in government. She always listened to what the ordinary people wanted.

Mo Mowlam has to be judged on what she achieved and how she handled her illness. She made a judgement not to tell people that she had a malignant tumour and decided to say that it was benign, she was probably right to make this judgement, because if she told one person she would have effectively told the world. She really wanted a job in government, so it was her decision to keep her illness a secret. Her mother, brother and sister did not know how serious her illness was. She was a major catalyst in the Peace Initiative and she may have been in a rush to get things done because of her illness.

Mo's mum Tina, was fond of telling people 'Mo is a born optimist. I always knew she would get somewhere. On the night that she was elected as an MP, she told me "Mum, this is what I've always wanted to do and I will do it well."'

Angela Atkin

Bibliography

The People's Peacemaker – 29th August 2005
The Search for Peace – BBC News
Coventry Evening Telegraph – Schoolgirl who went on to achieve so much
August 2005
Mo Mowlam – Wikipedia

Mehru Fitter

Mehru Fitter came to Britain in 1978 and has spent much of the time, until her retirement, as Coventry's Multi-Cultural Librarian. In her retirement she continues to work tirelessly for the people of Coventry. In 2003 she was awarded the MBE for her work.

When I first approached Mehru for permission to write this short biography, she got back to me and said she was willing to meet with me, but wrote 'I am not an interesting person.' I can testify that, after listening to Mehru's story for three hours, Mehru Fitter is a very interesting person! I leave you to make up your own minds.

Mehru's story begins in Mombasa in Kenya where she was born in 1943. She is the daughter of a civil servant who, at the age of eighteen, had emigrated from India to work in the law courts of Kenya. When Mehru was young, her father was posted to a small, attractive town called Eldoret. Mehru says, 'you will be very surprised to learn that all over Kenya we led segregated lives. The white ruling race had their own area and lived in very nice houses. They also had their own shops that we could not use.' Mehru's family lived in the Indian residential area and even in the Government quarter the toilet was outside. Africans were even worse off they lived in poorer houses with very few facilities. This was Apartheid, by any other name, in a British colony.

Mehru began school and loved it. 'We had brilliant teachers from India who although very strict we respected and adored. They gave us an excellent foundation. My mother was very determined that her five daughters were going to be well-educated. She had been forced to leave school at an early age and to ensure we did as well as possible she would get us up at five o'clock in the morning and test our tables and in the evening she set us homework. She was absolutely marvellous and highly stimulated. She taught herself and passed that knowledge on to us. For example, she was very keen on stories but with no library to call on she would use her needlework skills to embroider the folk tales she had heard and use these as a basis to tell stories to us. Sadly I haven't inherited her artistry.'

They lived in an area where everyone knew everyone else and parents

117

took pride in having well-behaved children. Teachers were very well respected and their praise was really sought after. Mehru has brilliant memories of her secondary school. 'We were very lucky. There were only twenty four pupils in each class which meant we had lots of personal attention. The head and teachers were very creative especially in dramatics, elocution contests and athletics. The last Head teacher was brilliant and really widened our horizons. He ensured we aimed for excellence and left school as *young ladies*.' With this stimulus, Mehru passed the Cambridge Overseas Scholarship at the age of fourteen. 'I had already made up my mind to be a teacher. Because of my age, my father had no option but to send me to India to study for my degree. I know my family were upset to see me leave and I was determined to be brave and managed not to shed a single tear when my father took me to board ship.' Unfortunately, Mehru's father died while she was in India.

Mehru enjoyed her four year stay in the newly independent India for a number reasons including meeting other Zoroastrians.* In Kenya there had not been any others for them to mix with and therefore explore their faith. Mehru also loved being educated in a country where literature by non-white authors was on the curriculum. Authors such as Tagore were very important. It was also very interesting to note that Forster's *A Passage to India* had been banned during the British rule.

At the age of nineteen Mehru received her degree. As a graduate she returned to Kenya and started teaching in a primary school. 'In those days if you had a degree, just as in England, it was thought you had the ability to teach your subject.' As she was a graduate, it was felt that she should teach in secondary schools and was transferred to a small town named Kisumu. It was a very nice town apart from the mosquitoes. On the day she reported for duty she found she would be teaching pupils only two or three years younger than her. An incident with the Deputy Head teacher illustrated this. When he saw her, he said she had better go home as there were no more school places on offer. He thought she was a pupil and would not believe her when she told him she was a teacher. 'I had to show him my letter of appointment before he believed me. I had the privilege of working under a remarkable Head teacher and an efficient deputy; they proved a formative influence on me. It was a thrilling experience to be a teacher. You were very highly respected and well-received. The public regarded us as *makers of the Nation.*'

After teaching for three or four years, Mehru felt that she should get a teaching qualification. Her sister, who had pursued a higher education teaching course in England, recommended that Mehru went to England to study. She undertook her Post Graduate Certificate of Education (PGCE) in English and Physical Education at the University of Newcastle-upon-Tyne. She clearly remembers what happened after her first physical education lesson in Kisumu. 'There was a long queue of parents who were concerned that their children had been over-exerted!' Mehru continued with her work, especially training the school athletes. They became known as the best athletes in Nyanza Province. Mehru was elated when the Kenyan runner, Kipchoge Keino, won his first gold medal. 'He has been an excellent role model. He set up an academy and has also fostered some seventeen to nineteen children,' she said, 'I was very glad when he received an honorary degree from Bristol University.'

At this time writers from non-white backgrounds were becoming internationally known and Mehru says she 'felt intense pride that Africa was becoming recognised on the map of the world's literature.'

Mehru was by this time Deputy Head teacher and also spent a lot of time working on the school library. The school did not have a budget for new material. 'There were only a few titles that were useful; the rest were inadequate or out of date. I realised the school needed money and I decided we just had to raise money. I made passion fruit juice and my mum made popcorn. I sold these during school break. In this way we started to raise lots of money. Local shopkeepers helped by giving me a very high discount and we managed to stock the library.

I then decided to go on a short course run by the British Council which covered *how to set up a library* and *classification of books*. I then introduced library induction for the whole school, covering the Dewey System and the arrangement of fiction. Library monitors were also appointed. There was a real thirst for knowledge; everyone wanted to read. Kenyans just love to read. For example, if someone has a newspaper, before it is thrown away you will find that tens of people may have read it.'

In 1978 Mehru's post was 'Africanised'. So Mehru came to England.

'Where else would I go? I had a British passport. However, I arrived at the same time that an aspiring politician named Margaret Thatcher was expressing her fear about Britain being *swamped by people with a different culture*. I remember looking for advice about getting a job and found a Citizen's Advice Bureau but with the speech against immigration ringing in my ears I wondered if I would be classed as a citizen. I paced up and down before mustering the courage to go inside. They pointed me towards the Inner London Education Authority (ILEA) where I got a job as a teacher.' Unfortunately, it was a time of school amalgamations and cut backs and so Mehru had to review her career.

Mehru was still very interested in Librarianship and her Head teacher explained that she could not really combine the two areas and she decided to train as a librarian at the School of Librarianship. Unfortunately, they charged her as an overseas student, which meant the fees were quite high. She applied to stay in a number of hostels but kept getting a refusal as they said that she was 'too old.' Luckily she applied to a hostel owned by Terence Driscoll. He had two hostels - in London and Surrey. She was amazed to learn that the Surrey hostel had been frequented by leading politicians from Africa and India. When she first met Terence, he asked why she had started her letter with 'I am a thirty four year old woman' because women as a rule did not give away their age. She explained about the refusals she had received and found him very welcoming and a 'brilliant landlord.' Because Mehru had to pay her own way through her course, she looked around for work. Terence was helpful and she started working in the kitchen, getting up at 5am to do two hours before going to college. She also helped with the evening meals for two hundred residents. 'I learnt to take care of my pennies. For example, I would walk to the next bus stop reminding myself that I would be saving 10p which would buy me a cup of tea. I did this for sixteen months!'

On the day Mehru finished her course she applied for a job in Southampton as a Community Librarian. She felt very lucky to be working under a city librarian who 'had this wonderful human quality, wanting nothing but the best for his employees.' After two years in Southampton, she saw an advert by Coventry Council asking for applications for a Multi-Cultural Librarian. She was successful and came to live in Coventry. 'The job description looked fine but the job grew bigger and bigger in size. It was, however, the right decision. Multi-culturalism was a challenging field. We were breaking new ground and there was very little advice to be had. We had to learn through trial and error.' The aim of Mehru's role was to ensure that all communities made maximum use of the library service. The question was 'how to sell the library to them. I decided if they wouldn't come to us we would have to go to them. I started to go to all events such as local community and religious festivals, making sure I exhibited our wares. Wherever there was something happening, I would be there. People were not, however, always impressed by pretty books. So I embarked on the practice of embellishing my displays with colourful artefacts, posters, etc. It was a hard sell to the managers – it was not the "done thing." Mehru remembers, with gratitude, the encouraging support of Roger Hughes, a City Librarian, who was a pillar of support and a tower of strength to multi-cultural library services.

'One of the festivals Foleshill Library participated in very regularly was Foleshill Festival. One year we decided to be very innovative and came up with the idea of a "Shop Window" competition around the theme –"It's Party time." The idea was for each shop to display their wares and promote a book from the library. One of the fashion shops had displayed a fashion book called *Sweet Sixteen*. This was a big success as we had numerous people asking for a copy of that book as well as copies of other books on display.

My visits to different lands widened my horizons considerably. Fortunately, my elder sister was the Head of an international school in Lesotho in Southern Africa and she used to attend international educational conferences, taking me along as her guest. We visited many countries. In Jamaica, I was very impressed with our reception; there were folk-singers at the airport. At our hotel we attended cultural evenings, all facilitated by young people. I was impressed at their pride in and knowledge of their national heroes and heroines. Coming from Africa, I noticed similarities between African and Caribbean art and handicrafts. The best workshop, and the one that was to have a lasting effect on my own practice, was a storytelling session, delivered by a superb Jamaican storyteller. It meant that I sometimes abandoned books and used lots of props to help me tell stories. This went down well with children. I was very impressed by the Aboriginal

Art I saw in Australia and the Maori culture of New Zealand. Also their stories were spell-binding. Wherever I travelled, I took the opportunity to bring back lots of artefacts which helped me arrange various days devoted to different cultures and communities in Coventry Libraries.'

Mehru provided very colourful exhibitions, but she was not happy with just this. 'It was my job to improve the library service for the Black and Minority Ethnic (BME) communities. There were a multitude of reasons for the lack of use and I had to rectify the situation. For example the book suppliers for minority languages would just send us what they wanted to. I realised that I needed to select the material and this is where my knowledge of languages came in handy. I was fluent in five languages: English, French, Gujarati, Hindi and Punjabi and had a good knowledge of literature from the developing world. However, I was not making much progress with the Bengali-reading community. I rectified the situation by learning Bengali, which helped me to communicate, as well as make a difference to our Bengali stock. My first library job was in Southampton, where I had good contacts with English for Speakers of Other Languages (ESOL) teachers. I forged similar links with Coventry teachers of ESOL and these links were very beneficial.'

Mehru achieved her aim of having high quality resources for adults learning English. It had been an uphill struggle. At that time it was felt that the adult literacy stock would serve the needs of adults learning English and she had to stress the difference between Adult Literacy, English as an Additional Language and English as a Foreign Language. She found that many adult learners of English could read English but the stumbling block was the lack of confidence in spoken English. To help, she built up a large stock of books accompanied by cassettes and CDs.

'I think the time has come to say that Coventry has the most welcoming communities that I have ever come across. I felt I was an honorary member of each community I serviced. For example I went to give a slide show for CARIBA at the West Indian Centre and felt part of their community straight away.

As we know, the City Council often has to make cuts. At some point we were threatened with the removal of all magazines. These were very important to our BME community members who decided to protest and raised a petition with five thousand signatures. They won a reprieve and said they had found the pen is often mightier than oral protests. Unfortunately, the majority [of the] community didn't protest and lost the facility for a while.

In the mid 80s Colin Scott became the Head of the Central Library and initiated a one day Multicultural Book Festival. We had book suppliers from all over the country and Benjamin Zephaniah was the main performer. Some seventy people came to hear him and as usual he was absolutely brilliant. We had spin offs from his performance. After hearing Benjamin Zephaniah, people indicated that they were very interested in poetry. Therefore, a Poetry Circle was set up at Foleshill Library. This developed as members indicated that they wanted opportunities to discuss short stories and fiction. So we started Readers Groups.

The first Multicultural Book Festival was a phenomenal success and this festival grew until we now have a festival taking place over three weeks with pre and post festival activities.' Mehru was one of the founder members of the organising committee of what became known as the Positive Images Multicultural Festival and Mehru is now secretary of the event which takes 10 months in the planning. She says, 'The best thing about the events is that they are free; they bring the voluntary, statutory and public sectors together and it is a community-led festival; the ideas come from the community. Every year we introduce a new feature with the majority of the suggestions coming from the member organisations.' Another festival Mehru has been involved in for several years is Coventry Women's Festival. This year (2011) she researched and developed an exhibition on *Women's Achievements in the Last One Hundred Years.*

Mehru acknowledges with pride her fantastic team who worked very hard with her to promote the library service. 'They were so committed that they were always looking for new ideas and opportunities for the promotion of the library service. They supported me in every way.' The Multicultural Library Service was held in high esteem at a national level and Mehru became a regular speaker at regional and national events. Unfortunately in 2003 Foleshill Library and its entire stock burned. 'We were devastated. It felt like the end of the world. However, we were really pleased to find out how much the communities cared for our service; they all rallied around and I received more phone calls than when I received my MBE. For one month the phone didn't stop ringing.'

The first award Mehru received was from the Library Association on the celebration of its centenary in 1998. 'It was given to me by Princess Anne. I was very nervous but she was a brilliant conversationalist. You felt that she was really interested in what you had to say. A few years later, in 2003, I received an envelope from the Prime Minister's office. I knew this was something serious but didn't open it until I got home that evening. When I saw that I had been nominated for the MBE, I felt disbelief. Then it began to sink in. What a huge surprise! I was asked to keep it secret but did inform my sister in Lesotho and my mother, who was living with me.

Unfortunately I didn't enjoy the day as well as I should have. I set out for the Palace in good time but a bus ahead of the taxi I was travelling in had caught fire and all traffic came to a standstill. I was worried about missing the ceremony. I spoke to the taxi driver and he was great. He drove over the pavement and got me to the ceremony one minute before the gates closed. The Queen was in Nigeria and so Prince Charles was handing out our awards. He came in accompanied by the Gurkhas as his guards. He was very pleasant but because of being late I was tense and nervous and just wanted to get back home. At the time I had no idea who had nominated me but about five years ago I was with someone who hinted that it was the various communities with whom I had worked. I was very pleased.

I was also surprised to receive The Glory of India Award from the India International Friendship Society. I went down to London to receive it but this was two days after the July 2005 bombings and it was difficult to feel happy.

Former residents of my home town, Kisumu, have formed an association which arranges reunions every few years. They too honoured me.'

Mehru Fitter.

124

Interfaith Work

Several years ago, because of her work with different communities, Mehru was contacted by the Coventry Multi-Faith Forum and as a Zoroastrian she was asked if she would join the Forum. 'This has been a huge part of my life and I found that I could transfer my skills from the library world to the multi-faith world. Every year we organise the Annual Peace Walk through the city. This has always been very successful. We are also involved in mounting numerous exhibitions. I am very pleased when people recognise that there are more things that bind us together than separate us. We feel that we play a huge part in enabling communities to bind together.

What has been very important has been the support we have received from Coventry City Council, which has recently set up a planning group for the celebration of festivals, with representation and input from the diverse communities of Coventry. For our first Inter-Faith Week we were overwhelmed by the support we received. We were noticed by the Interfaith Network for the United Kingdom and promoted as a model authority. As a member of the Forum, I attended the first ever Faith Guiding Course in Coventry and Warwickshire. It was very challenging but I received my level two certificate from the Institute of Tourist Guiding in June 2011. The award ceremony was held at the Sri Guru Singh Sabha Gurdwara in Cross Road. I think this proved it is never too late to learn and you are never too old!

As a result of being involved in interfaith work, I had the opportunity to learn more about my own faith. I think that if you understand your own faith, you are able to understand other faiths too. In 2009 I had the privilege of attending the 9th World Zoroastrian Congress in Dubai. It was a congress which I will never forget. It was very popular; taking place over four days, and was attended by seven hundred and fifty people from different countries and continents. Speakers said "it was the congress of a lifetime" and I am pleased to say that it was organised by a woman! The Congress put us in touch with one another and gave us first-hand knowledge of our achievements and the future aims of different countries' groups. I was impressed by the young people from Mumbai. They were involved with elderly people – ensuring they had someone to talk to, helping with shopping, etc., and showing that there is someone who cares.'

A Member of Parliament from Iran made a plea for more contact with Iran which was the birthplace of Zoroastrianism. Mehru also pointed out that it was here that the first women priests were trained. The Congress had also commissioned a special film illustrating the beginning of the faith and the reasons for the diaspora. 'It was really good to hear followers of other faiths make complimentary remarks about the Zoroastrian community's contribution in India. The congress catered for all ages and started many inter-continental friendships.

I am enjoying all the volunteering work that I do. It keeps me mentally stimulated. I have healthy links with Coventry Refugee Centre. I feel privileged to be associated with FolesHillfields Vision Project, which has done sterling work in bringing communities together and promoting Global Citizenship in schools. I'm particularly pleased that they give women a place to talk freely on a variety of issues.

I'm looking forward to 2012. Not only is it the Olympics year but also the year when Coventry Cathedral marks the 50th anniversary of its consecration. I am planning an exhibition on the theme of the Olympic Games looking at the Coventry dimension as well as the Olympic glories of the different countries that Coventry's communities have come from.'

Janice Wale

Acknowledgements

Our thanks must go to Mehru for all the hard work she has done and is continuing to do for the people of Coventry. We especially appreciate the time given from such a busy life to tell us this fascinating story.

*Zoroastrianism – Religion founded by Persian prophet Zoroaster in late 7th or early 6th centuries B.C.